SpringerBriefs in Criminology

AF709085

Policing

Series editor

M.R. Haberfeld
City University of New York
John Jay College of Criminal Justice
New York, NY, USA

More information about this series at http://www.springer.com/series/11179

Frank S. Pezzella

Hate Crime Statutes

A Public Policy and Law Enforcement Dilemma

Springer

Frank S. Pezzella
Department of Criminal Justice
John Jay College of Criminal Justice
New York, NY
USA

ISSN 2192-8533 ISSN 2192-8541 (electronic)
SpringerBriefs in Criminology
ISSN 2194-6213 ISSN 2194-6221 (electronic)
SpringerBriefs in Policing
ISBN 978-3-319-40840-8 ISBN 978-3-319-40842-2 (eBook)
DOI 10.1007/978-3-319-40842-2

Library of Congress Control Number: 2016942896

© The Author(s) 2017
This work is subject to copyright. All rights are reserved by the Publisher, whether the whole or part of the material is concerned, specifically the rights of translation, reprinting, reuse of illustrations, recitation, broadcasting, reproduction on microfilms or in any other physical way, and transmission or information storage and retrieval, electronic adaptation, computer software, or by similar or dissimilar methodology now known or hereafter developed.
The use of general descriptive names, registered names, trademarks, service marks, etc. in this publication does not imply, even in the absence of a specific statement, that such names are exempt from the relevant protective laws and regulations and therefore free for general use.
The publisher, the authors and the editors are safe to assume that the advice and information in this book are believed to be true and accurate at the date of publication. Neither the publisher nor the authors or the editors give a warranty, express or implied, with respect to the material contained herein or for any errors or omissions that may have been made.

Printed on acid-free paper

This Springer imprint is published by Springer Nature
The registered company is Springer International Publishing AG Switzerland

Contents

About the Author

Frank S. Pezzella Ph.D. (Criminal Justice, SUNY Albany) is Assistant Professor of Criminal Justice at John Jay College of Criminal Justice. His research interests include Race and Crime, Hate Crimes, and the influence of African American religiosity on the behavior of formerly incarcerated persons. This work was published in early 2014 in Springer's Journal of Religion and Health under the title "Religion and the Behavioral Health of Formerly Incarcerated Men." Prior to his current position he worked as an analyst and Deputy Chief Clerk for the NYS Unified Court System. He conducted research for legislative approval to implement community and problem-solving courts. Such specialized courts such as substance abuse, domestic violence, reentry, and mental health courts are now present throughout all 62 counties in New York State. Dr. Pezzella has also worked on the expansion and institutionalization of the original Manhattan Bail Project for Vera Institute's Pre-trial Services Agency [now the New York City Criminal Justice agency (CJA)] charged with assessing NYC defendants' eligibility for release on recognizance under evidence-based criteria that defendants will likely return to the jurisdiction of the court.

Chapter 1
Introduction

The impetus for writing this monograph is to illuminate the dilemmas that policymakers and first level judgement bias investigaors encounter attempting to enact and enforce contemporary hate crime statutes. Contemporary hate crime statutes are a well-intentioned legislative response to hate-motivated violence. However, they are not a novel idea and reflect reactions to hate-motivated behavior that have occurred over the last few decades. Earlier legislative responses to hate-motivated behavior can be detected during the reconstruction era of American history. During that period, numerous legislative acts were promulgated as a response to Ku Klux Klan centered violence such as lynching that was accompanied by cooperation, and often participation, of legal authorities (Baudouin 1997; Chalmers 1981; Petrosino 1999). In this respect, early civil rights statutes were enacted for the identical purpose of contemporary hate crime statutes; to protect citizens from the brutality of hate-motivated violence.

However, unlike the early civil rights statutes, contemporary hate crime statutes vary in the scope of protection, types of groups protected and the evidentiary criteria needed to assess bias motivation. Still, the civil right statutes represent the first legislative efforts, much like contemporary hate crime statutes, to address the growing problem of hate-motivated violence. In many respects, these nineteenth and twentieth century civil rights and hate crime statutes reflect the legacy of hate-motivated behavior in the United States.

Contemporary hate crime statutes have been drafted with more enforcement power and expanded federal and state jurisdiction. However, these statutes have been promulgated with significant constitutional and policy consequences that have generated paradoxical side effects including a series of social, enforcement, and legal dilemmas. Clearly, hate-motivated violence is not a new social phenomenon. However, statutes banning hate-motivated violence even with their victim exclusionary limitations are new. So why are state governments throughout the United States and Europe now enacting hate crime legislation? How does the history of hate-motivated violence correlate with contemporary hate-motivated violence? What are the challenges to enforce statutes proscribing hate-motivated violence?

© The Author(s) 2017

F.S. Pezzella, *Hate Crime Statutes*, SpringerBriefs in Policing,
DOI 10.1007/978-3-319-40842-2_1

These are questions that are explored in this monograph. The monograph begins in this introductory chapter with a discussion of the emotion of hate as a precursor to defining hate and hate crime statutes and the message from hate offenders. The chapter concludes with a discussion of the pragmatic issues that cloud our understanding of the nature and the extent of the hate crime problem in contemporary America. Next, Chap. 2 presents a discussion on the history of hate in America that focuses on four significant eras that are precursors to the most prevalent contemporary bias victimization types. Chapter 3 underscores the argument in favor of hate crime statutes delineating the variation in injuries between bias and comparable nonbias crimes. Chapter 4 describes offender, victim and situational characteristic unique to the bias crime incident incorporating findings from UCR, National Incident-Based Reporting System (NIBRS) and National Crime Victimization (NCVS) Studies. Chapter 5 reviews contemporary federal and state legislative responses to hate crimes. The chapter focuses on the variation in protected groups across the states and the differences in evidentiary criteria required to establish bias motivation. Chapter 6 illuminates the constitutional and unintended policy issues that hate crime statutes present particularly to first level bias judgement and responding police officers and prosecutors. Chapter 7 uncovers the law enforcement and prosecution dilemma as encountered by the first level responding police officer or bias investigator and the prosecutor responsible for establishing bias motivation beyond a reasonable doubt. Finally, Chap. 8 summarizes these issues and suggests an enhanced prevention policy through public awareness and education about the harms of hate. In addition, best practices for assessing and proving bias motivation for police agencies are discussed.

Historic and Contemporary Hate Crime Statutes

In 1990 when President Reagan and the U.S. Congress enacted the Hate Crime Statistics act (HCSA), it marked the beginning of the federal government's official recognition of the unique harm of hate crimes in the twentieth century (Gerstenfeld 2013). Essentially, the purpose of the HCSA of 1990 (28 U.S.C. 534) was to authorize the Federal Bureau of Investigation Uniform Crime Reporting Program (UCR) to collect and analyze data from federal and state voluntarily participating police agencies to assess the nature and scope of hate crimes. Today, the UCR hate crime reporting program provides annual statistics on the prevalence of hate crimes and also special reports demonstrating trends in hate-motivated violence. Although the HCSA of 1990 did not include an enforcement provision, the authorization to collect hate crime prevalence rates from federal, state and local police agencies reflected concern about the unique consequences of hate crimes. While the enactment of the thirteenth, fourteenth and fifteenth amendments and subsequent civil rights bills sought to abolish slavery, provide equal protection of the law and ensure voting and other civil right, these legislative initiatives were very limited in jurisdiction and statutory power to prosecute hate-motivated violence.[1] Therefore, the HSCA of 1990 was somewhat unique in that it not only authorized collection and analysis of hate crime prevalence, it also defined the criminal conduct that constituted a hate crime. According to the HCSA of 1990 definition, hate crimes are acts that manifest evidence of prejudice based on actual or perceived race, religion, sexual orientation or ethnicity.

A few scholars have argued that statutory definitions of hate crimes such as the HCSA definition are quite narrow because they focus on bias-motivated violence against preselected and predefined vulnerable groups (Petrosino 1999; Chakraborti 2014; Mason-Bish 2014). Arguably, hate conduct is not limited to acts of violence against these statutory exclusive groups. Petrosino (1999) asserted that statutory definitions of hate crimes reflect a temporal dimension of bias-motivated conduct that proscribes present and future hate-motivated behavior. However, hate-motivated incidents of comparable magnitude throughout American history were not considered hate crimes because they were considered normative and consistent with the prevalent attitudes during that era. Further, if you redefine hate crime outside of statutory definitions, from a deontological perspective, solely on the conduct of hate-motivated violence, then the origin of hate crimes in America can be dated back to the colonial era (Chen 2000). Consider the prevalence of lynching primarily African-Americans; the infamous trail of tears so titled to describe the atrocities against Native Americans forced to relocate to reservations. Likewise, recall the history of anti-Semitism, pogroms and violence against Jews both in America and Europe. Moreover, the history of gay bashing in the United States and discrimination and persecution against people of alternative sex orientations prevalent throughout the world in the first half of the twentieth century. Also, the history of persecution and bias-motivated violence against gypsies and travelers throughout Europe. Clearly, these artifacts of world history provide evidence that crimes based on hate has existed for centuries. The legacy of hate crimes reflects the history of mans inhumanity against man. Interesting, Chakraborti (2014) contends that we should reframe the boundaries of who we consider to be victims of hate crimes to include other victims groups. Similarly, Mason-Bish (2014) argued that the silo approach of including some victim groups under the umbrella of protection that "shout louder" about the harm of hate to their interest group in lieu of others excludes important segments of victims. These are important issues because they either restrict or extend our conceptualization of the prevalence and severity of hate-motivated violence. However, before statutory definitions of hate are examined, we should first analyze the emotion of hate and then endeavor to understand the difficulty in conceptualizing the notion of hate crime.

[1]Federal civil rights statutes limitations included: a narrow view of the interstate commerce clause; language primarily directed towards limiting the Ku Klux Klan violence; limited federalism and deference to states for criminal prosecution; and the absence of resources to enforce hate crime laws.

The Emotion of Hate

What is it about hate that when expressed in criminal conduct that it is deemed so detrimental that sanctions more severe than those applied to non-hate-motivated crime are necessary? To address this question, understanding the dimensions of hate is critical. It is important to note that hate, like other mental states, is an emotion. Allport (1954) defined the emotion of hate as:

> An enduring organization of aggressive impulses towards a person or towards a class of persons. Since it is composed of habitual bitter feelings and accusatory thought, it constitutes a stubborn structure in the mental-emotional life of the individual. By its very nature, hate is extra-punitive, which means that the hater is sure the fault lies in the object of his hate. So long as he believes this he will not feel guilty for his uncharitable state of mind (p. 363)

In terms of intensity, hate is comparable to rage or its opposite, love and in this regard it is quite complex. Hate is not just the absence of objectivity or an attitude. Hate requires a direct object, against another human being, with which loathing is directed towards. The emotion of hate carries the intention of ill will, malevolence, detestation or enmity toward another human being for some perceived rational, often irrational reason (Gaylin 2004). Hate is quite unique because of its intensity. It is this intensity that distinguishes hate from attitudinal attributes such as bigotry, prejudice and bias that often accompanies it. Bigotry merely describes a level of intolerance and prejudice of the person. Hate can also be distinguished from prejudice. Allport (1954) described prejudice as an attitude: "an avertive or hostile attitude towards a person who belongs to a group, simply because he belongs to that group, and is therefore presumed to have objectionable qualities ascribed to that group" (p. 7). Still, prejudice cannot rival the emotion of hate because it is qualitatively and arguably, quantitatively different than hate because of its intensity. Unlike other negative emotions such as disappointment, dislike, or disdain, hate is a much more in-depth ill regard for another person or persons.

Although used interchangeably with the term bias throughout hate crime scholarship, the emotional intensity of hate and conduct reflecting bias may vary considerably. Bias, much like bigotry, suggests the absence of objectivity. As a description of the type of unlawful conduct proscribed in statutes both hate and bias crimes imply intolerance, ill will and prejudice toward another person or particular group. When considered separately, attitudes reflecting bigotry, prejudice and or bias vary from the raw intensity of the emotion of hate. However, when these attitudes are combined with the emotional intensity of hate, the resulting conduct creates an extremely undesirable set of victim circumstances and societal outcomes. Gaylin (2004) and the 2015 UCR hate crime data collection guidelines for assessing bias motivation indicators posit that biased conduct, bigotry and prejudice are preliminary indicators of, and often precursors to, hate-motivated violence.[2]

---

[2]See Appendix for List of FBI bias indicators.

The Problem of Defining Hate Crimes

So how exactly do we define a hate crime? The answer to this question varies according to the whether hate crimes are observed from a statutory or deontological perspective (Petrosino 1999). Hate crime scholars have offered substantial variations in definitions which to a large extent has made the problem of hate motivated violence difficult to conceptualize. Incorporating a deontological perspective, Petrosino (1999) conceptualized a definition with two critical elements. First, "the victimization of minorities due to their racial or ethnic identity by members of the majority; secondly, whether legal authorities of that time would have responded to the acts in a similar fashion if victims were White Anglo-Saxon protestant" (p. 5). Petrosino's (1999) definition underscores the power imbalance between majority and minority groups within the context of perpetrator and victim relationship and considers the historical origins of hate-motivated behavior. Incorporating this type of deontological definition links hate crimes against historically victimized groups to the most prevalent types of contemporary victimizations.

However, Lawrence (2009) distinguished "bias" from "hate" crimes suggesting that it is not the offender's hatred per se but his bias or prejudice towards the victim. He defined a bias crime as "a crime committed as an act of prejudice" (p. 9). Interestingly, he clarified that "bias crimes are crimes in which distinct identifying characteristics of the victim are critical to the choice of the victim".... "A bias crime occurs not because the victim is who he is, rather because the victim is what he is" (p. 9). Alternatively, Perry (2001) much like Petrosino (1999) contextualized the power imbalance between majority and minority group members in her definition of hate crime. She posited hate crimes as:

> An act of violence and intimidation, usually directed toward already stigmatized and marginalized groups. As such, it is a mechanism of power, intended to reaffirm the precarious hierarchies that characterize a given social order. It attempts to recreate simultaneously the threatened, (real or imagined) hegemony of the perpetrator's group and the appropriate subordinate identity of the victim's group (p. 10)

Jacobs and Potter's (1998) definition omitted reference to the power imbalance, simply suggesting hate crime "refers to criminal conduct motivated by prejudice" (p. 11). Similarly, Gerstenfeld (2013) defined hate crime: "the simplest definition of a hate crime is an criminal act that is motivated in part, by group affiliation of the victims" (p. 11). It is important to note that Lawrence (2009), Jacobs and Potter (1998) and Gerstenfeld (2013) incorporate codified definitions of "criminal conduct" or a "criminal act" to define a hate crime. However, acts of violence against persons other than white were largely not considered a criminal act throughout most of American history (Petrosino 1999). Significantly, deontological definitions of hate crimes allow for consideration of the legacy of hate in the past to that of the present. As a result, it is possible to attain a sense of the historical nature of hate crimes so that future policy strategies can consider systematically the deep roots of hate crimes that are firmly entrenched within American culture.

Perhaps the most inclusive definition of hate crimes are acts of violence against a person because their group membership. This definition incorporates Chakraborti's (2014) call to expand the boundaries of those we consider victims and Mason-Bish (2014) criticism of the silo approach to defining victims based on interest groups that shout the loudest. As mentioned, contemporary definitions of hate crimes are largely statutorily defined with preselected vulnerable victim groups. Consequently, statutory definitions depend on the jurisdiction where hate motivated incidents happen. Therefore, the conduct that constitutes a hate crime, although identical to a parallel conventional crime, varies based on the membership status of the victim and the jurisdiction where the incident occurred; and conceivably whether federal hate crime laws were violated.

In 2016, 46 states and the federal have enacted hate crime legislation that incorporate definitions that vary significantly with respect to which groups are predefined as vulnerable and warrant special protection. Some states offer race, ethnicity, and religious protection; other states offer protection based on race, ethnicity, religion, gender, sex and gender orientation. Almost all states that have promulgated state hate crime statutes include, at a minimum, race, religion, and national origin (ethnicity), the original civil rights groups protected under several earlier civil rights statutes[3] (Gerstenfeld 2013). In addition to race, religion, and national origin, of the 46 states with state hate crime statutory provisions, 31 include sex orientation; 27 include gender; 31 include disability; 13 include transgender; 13 include age; and 5 include political affiliation (www.adl.org). Four states including Arkansas, Georgia, Indiana, and South Carolina have not promulgated any legislation that consider special status groups eligible for state hate crime protection. Statutes also vary in the evidentiary requirements needed to establish the hate or bias motivation necessary for a conviction. Some states follow the "discriminatory selection" model that requires victim selection "because of" membership in a previously defined protected status group. Other states require evidence of "racial animus" towards predefined protected group as the criteria for a hate crime conviction. Clearly such provincial definitions and variation in evidentiary requirements present serious problems for conceptualizing and measuring the incidence and prevalemce of hate crime. It is exactly this kind of ambiguity that creates policy and enforcement dilemmas that challenge the purpose of hate crime legislation.

Why has hate crime statutes proliferated over the last two and a half decades in the United States? Arguably, hate crime statutes reflect the consensus of societal values regarding the severity and seriousness of certain types of conduct (Lawrence 2002). To this extent, hate crimes statutes underscore society's consensus and demarcation of bias-motivated criminal behaviors as qualitatively different and likely to undermine democratic societal values. In addition, research on the social

---

[3]Inclusive of the first Civil Rights Act in 1871 with specific provision provided for in 18 U.S.C. 241; 18 U.S.C. 242; 42 U.S.C. 1983 and a century later 18 U.S.C. sec 245.

impact of hate crime victimizations have found hate crimes are increasingly likely to influence retaliatory acts of hate (McDevitt et al. 2002, 18 U.S. 249). Consequently, societal cohesion, and safety are undermined with polarizations effects likely to foster intergroup conflict. Hate crimes have also been cited as more injurious than comparable non-hate-motivated crimes garnering multidimensional injuries to victims (Berrill 1990; Iganski and lagou 2014; Pezzella and Fetzer 2015). It is for these reasons that hate or bias-motivated conduct has evolved as outlawed behavior both nationally and internationally.

The Putative Message from Hate Offenders

The message from hate offenders to direct and vicarious victims is critical to understanding the nature of hate victimizations. Historically and contemporarily, hate offenders intend to communicate their belief of group superiority and entitlement over primary and distal secondary victims. Gerstenfeld (2013) noted the symbolic messages and clarity of the hate act: "the messages of a swastika or a burning cross are clear": "you're not wanted here. You're not valuable human beings. We are powerful and you should fear us. Do not assert yourself or you will be harmed" (p. 27).

Other scholars assert the hate message is also sent to society at large for its maximum repressive effects on intergroup trust and democratic ideals of equality and inclusion. According to Lim (2009) and Perry and Alvi (2012) the hate message is often received with the full effect of the offender's intentions. Both direct and vicarious victims feel a sense of vulnerability as a result of their interchangeability. McDevitt et al. (2001) defined victim interchangeability as "any individual who possesses or perceived to possess a specific trait could be a target" (p. 698). Consequently, the possibility of victim interchangeability causes vicarious victims that are proximally close to the primary victim to feel the constant threat of violence. Therefore, vicarious victims receive the message from hate offenders and are always in fear. Ultimately, the purpose of the message to change and safeguard their behavior is accepted and the potential for a bias victimization is internalized as normative as a constant threat of future violence.

Arguably, one of the reasons why hate messages are so effectively delivered is because hate crimes remind victims of centuries old terror of past hate atrocities potentially emerging into the present as an immediate and distinct threat (Boeckmann and Turpin-Petrosino 2002; Herek et al. 2002; Lim 2009; Perry and Alvi 2012). African-American victims are reminded of the four hundred years of slavery and the American history of lynching; Jews are reminded of pogroms in Europe and the holocaust; and LGBT persons are made to recall the brutalization of victims particularly during the first half of the twentieth century. The messianic nature of hate crimes is one of the reasons scholars consider hate crimes uniquely lethal.

The Extent of the Problem

There is considerable uncertainty about the prevalence of hate crimes in the United States because accurate estimations are difficult to assess. Several converging factors contribute to this uncertainty that render official reports of hate crimes incidents largely underestimated. These include victim underreporting (BJA 1997), state variations in groups eligible for protection (Torres 1999), and police misclassification and underreporting of hate crimes (Levin 2002).

Notwithstanding these limitations, a major benefit of collecting official hate data is the developing capacity to establish baseline prevalence rates to track trends in hate-motivated violence. In the United States, hate crime prevalence rates are derived from three official sources including the Uniform Form Crime Report (UCR), the National Incident-Based Reporting System (NIBRS),[4] and the National Crime Victimization Survey (NCVS). The NCVS has been collecting data on hate crime victimizations since 2003. Essentially, 60,000 households are surveyed every six months to assess the rate of crime victimizations to individuals or households. Unlike the UCR, the NCVS does not include murder, non-negligent manslaughter, intimidation, arson, vandalism, and crimes against institutions. However, it does include UCR crimes known and unknown to the police. Between these three sources, the most prevalent types of victimization and the nature of estimation problem can be assessed.

Figure 1 illustrates trends depicting the annual number of single bias incidents, victims, and police participating agencies in the hate crime reporting program since 1994. The trend line illustrates a baseline number of 5932 single bias-motivated incidents reported in 1994 and concludes with 5462 single bias-motivated incidents in 2014. Further observations of the trend line reveal substantial variation in hate-motivated incidents over the decades of hate crime reporting. Hate crime incidents appear to have inclined and declined several times through the period peaking in 2001 with a total of 9721 of hate crime incidents reflecting a spike in anti-Muslim hate crimes after 9/11.

Figure 1 also illustrates the growth in the number of participating police agencies over the 25 year period. The number of police participating police agencies have increased from 2771 in 1991 (not shown in trend line) to 15,494 in 2014 representing 93 % of the U.S. Population (UCR 2015). However, it is important to note that police agency participation in the hate crime reporting program has been estimated at only 75 % of the 18,000 police agencies that participate in the general UCR program (ADL 2012; Cronin et al. 2007; Torres 1999). Therefore, nearly 4500 or 25 % of participating UCR police agencies do not participate and consequently do not report hate crimes pursuant to the HCSA of 1990. As a result, UCR

[4]NIBRS, a subdivision of the UCR program collects and provides rich incident level data on the date, time, place, offender and victim and situational characteristics in NIBRS participating municipalities; however NIBRS does not reflect a representative sampling of crime in the U.S.

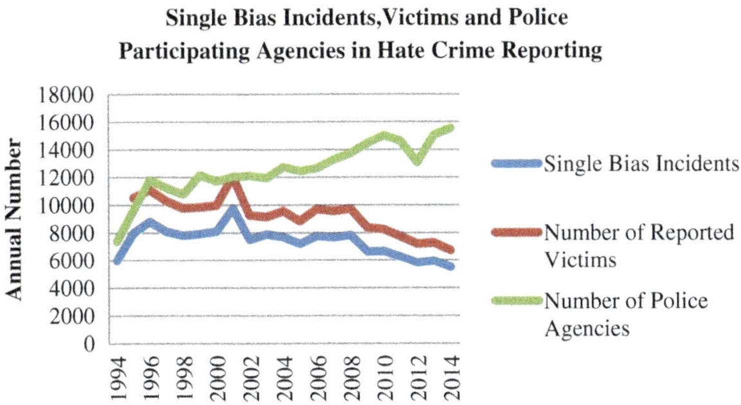

Fig. 1 Trendline depicting single bias incidents, Victims, and Police Participating Agencies in hate crime reporting program

annual reports of hate crimes begin with this severe underestimation derived from approximately 4500 non-participating police jurisdictions.

Further, it is interesting to note that while the number of participating police agencies in the hate crime reporting program has grown exponentially since 1991, the annual number of reported hate crimes has not kept pace. More specifically, the total number of reported single and multiple bias crime incidents reports reflect only a small increase over the 25 years period of official hate crime reporting. This seems counterintuitive to the expectation that annual rates of police reported hate crimes would, at a minimum, increase somewhat proportionally to the increase in the number of participating police agencies. Interestingly, a closer look at this paradox revealed that 90 % of police agencies that participate in the UCR hate crime reporting program reported "zero" number of hate crimes. Consequently, the substantial majority (90 %), of participating police agencies have not reported a single hate crime.

The likelihood of police underreporting is further supported by the fact that the number of protected groups under state hate crime legislation have increased as more and more states have enacted hate crime legislation over the last few decades. Recall, the HCSA of 1990 initially defined hate crimes as "acts that manifest evidence of prejudice based on race, religion, disability, sex orientation or ethnicity" However, in 2004 and 2009 the number of status groups redefined as eligible for federal hate crime protection was expanded to include disability (2004) and then gender, gender identity (2009), respectively. Again, the small increase in reported hate crimes over the past few decades is counterintuitive in light of the expansion of protected groups and the burgeoning number of states that have enacted hate crime legislation. Also, recall hate crime victims outside of these federally protected groups are not included (Chakraborti 2014; Mason-Bish 2014) as well as the victims that may be included under state but not federal defintions of a protected hate crime vulnerable group. Some states incorporate statutory definitions that include status groups over and beyond the federal definition. These victims are not included in official estimates further obfuscating annual reports of hate crime prevalence.

Contributing further to the estimation issues, police agencies within these states are required to limit or expand their reporting pursuant to the UCR federal definition of protected groups. For example, states that incorporate hate crimes status protection because of age (13 states), or political affiliation (5 states) are not included in the UCR annual hate crime report. Clearly, it would not be inappropriate to construe that the number of officially reported hate crimes falls far short and thus contributes to a sizable dark figure of hate crime under reporting.

One way to illuminate the level of underreporting of hate crimes is to examine the scale of victimization accounts of hate crimes. The NCVS uses the same UCR definition of hate crime that was redefined in 2009 under the Mathew Shepard and Robert Byrd, Jr. Hate Crime Prevention Act (18 U.S. 249). According to a special NCVS report, 2012 witnessed the highest number of hate crime victimizations ever, (293,790) reflecting a 32 % increase over the number of victimizations in 2005 (223,060). Moreover, this increase in victim reported hate crimes corresponds to a stable and considerable rate of hate violence. Of the 223,060 hate crime victimizations reported in 2005, 198,000 (89 %) were violent victimizations involving rape, sexual assault, robbery, aggravated assault or simple assault. By 2012, of the 293,790 hate crime victimizations reported, 263,540 (90 %) were similar violent victimizations reflecting a consistent rate of hate violence (Wilson 2014). Clearly, given the scale of victimization accounts, official contemporary estimates of the nature and prevalence of hate crimes starts with a statistical disability that gives rise to a dark figure of hate crime under reporting. More importantly, if victim reports are credible, the extent of the problem of hate crimes is extremely more serious than the hate crime reporting program reflects. The disparity between victim and police reports and the factors contributing to underreporting warrants scrutiny.

Victim Under Reporting

Sadly, another significant factor contributing to inaccurate estimates of hate crimes is the under reporting by many of the arguably marginalized status groups currently protected under the Matthew Shepard and Robert Byrd Jr. Hate Crime Prevention Act of 2009. Marginalized groups such as African-Americans or members of the Lesbian, Gay, Transgender and Queer (LGBTQ) communities are often reluctant to report their victimization because of distrust, fear or strained relationships with law enforcement (BJA 1997; Nolan and Akiyama 1999; McDevitt et al. 2002). In addition, victims often fear retaliation from perpetrators and the potential for secondary victimization by police. Another problem particularly unique to immigrants may be their inability to speak English or their status as undocumented aliens that would increase their risk for deportation (BJA 1997). In addition, in many Asian cultures, being a victim of a bias-motivated crime carries a stigma that also brings shame to their family and perceived as a degrading and humiliating experience. In these cases, filing a report will expose them to further humiliation (BJA 1997).

Finally, recent research on hate crime victimization of the disabled has uncovered physical access, institutional and social barriers that impede disabled hate crime victims from reporting. Thorneycroft and Asquith (2015) found that hate crimes were often so normative to disabled hate crime victims that they were frequently unaware that they were victims of hate-motivated violence. Worse, Sin et al. (2009) found that victims of disabled motivated hate crimes were often advised not to report particularly when the disabled victim has a learning disability. Victim underreporting is a serious factor that serves to confound our understanding of the prevalence of hate crimes. In addition, police underreporting and police misclassification decisions also contribute to the problem. The discussion of police underreporting and misclassification decisions are reserved for Chap. 7 wherein the dilemmas encountered by first responding police officers to the bias incident are presented. Finally, looking beyond the time period of contemporary hate crime statutes indicates continuity between past and present particularly for historic victims of hate that can be predicted as the most prevalent victims today. Policies designed to deter hate crimes should begin with understanding the legacy and typology of hate crime in the United States.

References

ADL. (2012). Hate crime laws.

Allport, G. W. (1954). *The nature of prejudice*. Cambridge, MA: Addison Wesley.

Baudouin, R. (1997). *The Ku Klux Klan: A history of racism and violence* (5th ed.). Montgomery, Al: Southern Poverty Law center.

Berrill, K. T. (1990). Anti-gay violence and victimization in the United States an overview. *Journal of Interpersonal Violence, 5*(3), 274–294.

Boeckmann, R. J., & Turpin-Petrosino, C. (2002). Understanding the harm of hate crime. *Journal of Social Issues, 58*(2), 207–225.

BJA, (1997). A Policymaker's guide to hate crimes-national criminal justice reference service https://www.ncjrs.gov/…162.

Chakraborti, N. (2014). Framing the boundaries of hate crime. *The Routledge International Handbook on Hate Crime, 13*.

Chalmers, D. M. (1981). *Hooded Americanism: The history of the Ku Klux Klan*. Duke University Press.

Chen, T. Y. L. (2000). Hate violence as border patrol: An Asian American theory of hate violence. *Asian LJ, 7*, 69.

Criminal Justice Information Services, Division of Uniform Crime Reporting program, (2015). Hate crime data collection guidelines and training manual, Version 2.0.

Cronin, S. W., McDevitt, J., Farrell, A., & Nolan, J. J. (2007). Bias-crime reporting organizational responses to ambiguity, uncertainty, and infrequency in eight police departments. *American Behavioral Scientist, 51*(2), 213–231.

Gaylin, W. (2004). *Hatred: The psychological descent into violence*. New York: Public Affairs.

Gerstenfeld, P. B. (2013). *Hate crimes: Causes, controls, and controversies*. Sage.

Herek, G. M., Cogan, J. C., & Gillis, J. R. (2002). Victim experiences in hate crimes based on sexual orientation. *Journal of Social Issues, 58*(2), 319–339.

Iganski, P., & Lagou, S. (2014). The personal injuries of 'hate crime'. *The Routledge International Handbook on Hate Crime*, pp 34–46.

Jacobs, J. B., & Potter, K. (1998). *Hate crimes: Criminal law and identity politics* (Vol. 67). New York: Oxford University Press.

Lawrence, F. M. (2002). *Racial violence on a 'small island': Bias crime in a multicultural society*. Should Hate be Punished as a Crime: The Hate Debate.

Lawrence, F. M. (2009). *Punishing hate: Bias crimes under American law*. Harvard University Press.

Levin, B. (2002). From slavery to hate crime laws: The emergence of race and status-based protection in American criminal law. *Journal of Social Issues*, *58*(2), 227–245.

Lim, H. A. (2009). Beyond the immediate victim: Understanding hate crimes as message crimes. *Hate crimes: The consequences of hate crime, 2*, 107–222.

Mason-Bish, H. (2014). Beyond the Silo. *The Routledge International Handbook on Hate Crime*, 24.

McDevitt, J., Balboni, J., Garcia, L., & Gu, J. (2001). Consequences for victims: A comparison of bias and non-bias-motivated assaults. *American Behavioral Scientist*, *45*(4), 697–713.

McDevitt, J., Levin, J., & Bennett, S. (2002). Hate crime offenders: An expanded typology. *Journal of Social Issues, 58*(2), 303–317.

Nolan, J. J., & Akijama, Y. (1999). An analysis of factors that affect law enforcement participation in hate crime reporting. *Journal of Contemporary Criminal Justice, 15*(1), 111–127.

Perry, B. (2001). *In the name of hate: Understanding hate crimes*. Psychology Press.

Perry, B., & Alvi, S. (2012). 'We are all vulnerable' The in terrorem effects of hate crimes. *International Review of Victimology, 18(*1), 57–71.

Petrosino, C. (1999). Connecting the past to the future hate crime in America. *Journal of Contemporary Criminal Justice, 15*(1), 22–47.

Pezzella, F. S., & Fetzer, M. D. (2015). The likelihood of injury among bias crimes: An analysis of general and specific bias types. *Journal of Interpersonal Violence*, 0886260515586374.

Sin, C. H., Hedges, A., Cook, C., Mguni, N., & Comber, N. (2009). Disabled people's experiences of targeted violence and hostility. *Manchester: Equality and Human Rights Commission*.

Thorneycroft, R., & Asquith, N. L. (2015). The dark figure of disablist violence. *The Howard Journal of Criminal Justice, 54*(5), 489–507.

Torres, S. (1999). Hate crimes against African Americans the extent of the problem. *Journal of Contemporary Criminal Justice, 15*(1), 48–63.

Wilson, M. M. (2014). Bureau of Justice Statistics, US Dept. of Justice, Office of Justice Programs, United States of America. Hate crime victimization, 2004–2012—Statistical tables.

Chapter 2
The Legacy of Hate Crimes in American History

Hate motivated violence is steeped in both American and European culture and history. In Europe, hate victim groups such as Roma, Gypsies, Travelers, and Jews have experienced centuries of hate motivated violence. Similarly in American history, African-Americans, Hispanics, Native Americans, Jews and lesbian, gay, bisexual, transgendered, and queers persons and generally non-white persons have often been the victims of prejudice and hate-motivated violence (Petrosino 1999). Hate crimes in the United States can be dated back to colonial America. Conceivably, establishing a historical timeline between past and present hate crimes can assist in developing public policy that includes an understanding of the origins and nature of hate victimizations. Recall one of the problems with using statutory definitions of hate crimes is the implicit assumption that hate crimes were either nonexistent or not a serious problem before the enactment of hate crime legislation (Petrosino 1999). Petrosino (1999) posited the predominance of American jurisprudence throughout history reflects the political nature of lawmaking and its functional role to keep powerless groups from making moral, ethical, and legal claims of hate crimes. In this regard, two factors contribute to our misunderstanding of the origins and nature of hate victimizations. First, normative values of past eras denied personhood to hate crime victims because of the absence of constitutional, statutory, and legal redress for victims. Second, the U.S. government itself has held a complicit and direct role in perpetrating hate crimes (Petrosino 1999). Consider the legacy of four centuries of slavery (King et al. 2009); the near genocide of the Yuki and Cheyenne Indian (Petrosino 1999); law enforcement tolerance and participation in lynching (Wells-Barnett 1969); and hate crimes perpetrated against Asian Immigrants (Chen 2000). In many state constitutions, non-white races and ethnicities were disallowed full legal redress in matters that accused Whites persons. The net effect of this type of historical amnesia has been that the nature and severity of hate crime victimizations has not been recognized because racism and xenophobia was largely, normative. Hate crime atrocities against non-white persons did not alarm the consciousness of citizens because the internal ethical and moral

© The Author(s) 2017

F.S. Pezzella, *Hate Crime Statutes*, SpringerBriefs in Policing,
DOI 10.1007/978-3-319-40842-2_2

compass throughout most of American history guaranteed rights, privileges, and protection of personhood only to White citizens.

Here, we recall the history of hate crimes in America and Europe to provide both a context and continuity between past and the present hate motivated violence. Arguably, historical accounts of hate-motivated violence throughout American history may serve to explain why certain hate-motivated behaviors and types of victimizations continue to be so prevalent and robust within American culture over the last three centuries. (Chen 2000). By no means exhaustive, four significant eras of hate-motivated violence is presented to contextualize our understanding of contemporary hate crimes.

Interestingly, when we recount hate victimization throughout American history, it is not just ironic that the most prevalent bias victimization categories today are race, religion, and sex orientation. Even more interesting, and not so ironic, within these generalized categories, history provides evidence of specific types of hate that have sustained prevalence over time. Recall the history of American lynching of African-Americans; racial atrocities that paralleled the birth and rebirths of the Ku Klux Klan; anti-Semitism and the holocaust; and the history of gay and lesbian bashing. These episodes of hate violence are historically significant and not so ironically link to contemporary prevalence of historic and specific types of bias.

American Lynching

The practice of lynching in American history is perhaps the most obvious evidence of the historical continuity between hate-motivated violence in the past and contemporary hate crimes (Gabbidon and Greene 2016). Lynching was quite prevalent during the nineteenth and early twentieth century. Comparable to contemporary hate crimes, lynching served the same purpose as defined by sociologist Oliver Cox (1945). Cox (1945) defined "lynching" as:

> an act of homicidal aggression committed by one people against another through mob action for the purpose of suppressing either some tendency in the later to rise from an accommodated position of subordination or for subjugating them further to some lower social status. (p. 576)

Named after Charles Lynch during the nineteenth century, lynching was practiced in the American Revolutionary war when vigilante patriots lynched loyalist. Moreover, lynching was prevalent in the history of the American West where horse and cattle thieves, murderers, claim jumpers, and people of Hispanic descent were lynched (Jacobs and Potter 1998). However, lynching became more prominent and a settled form of unofficial justice after the civil war, particularly when it was directed at African-American victims (Chalmers 1981; Howard 2005). Both the threat of lynching and lynching prevented by friendly White persons served to maintain White dominance. Petrosino (1999) described lynching as the execution of an accused individual without due process of law. However, the history of lynching in the United States indicates that it is very much more purposeful and complex. Lynching, to a large extent, is an exemplary and symbolic act. Cox (1945) noted that it is an attack principally against all African-Americans in some community rather than against an individual African-American. Its purpose was not to eliminate dangerous individuals from society, but to make the occasion as impressive as possible to the entire population of both African-Americans and Whites. In essence, it was designed to reaffirm White dominance.

The practice of lynching often occurred with the tacit approval of legal authorities. Occurring primarily in areas where discrimination and prejudice was quite prominent, the administrative judicial machinery frequently facilitated the act of lynching (Cox 1945). Lynching for all intents and purposes was not a crime in the south during the era of lynching and offenders who practiced lynching were not viewed as criminals (Gabbidon and Greene 2016). To be a crime, lynching had to be considered an offence against the state. However, the predominant assumptions and prevalent thinking of the community during the era of lynching did not consider lynching against the law. To this point, Raper (1933) asserted:

> Mobs do not come out of nowhere; they are the logical outgrowths of dominant assumptions and prevalent thinking. Lynchings are not the work of men suddenly possessed of strange madness; they are the logical issue of prejudice and lack of respect for law and personality. (p. 47)

Consequently, lynch mobs seldom feared legal repercussions. Although lynching was never statutorily advocated, it was taken for granted in the south that Whites could use force against any African-American who became overbearing. Raper (1933) further noted that the rationale for lynching rested on the assumption of the unlimited rights of White men and the absence of any rights on the part of African-Americans. Therefore, it was not uncommon for African-Americans to be taken from police custody or from a courtroom because of the assumption that the law was not available to African-Americans because they were not equal in standing to White persons. Further, lynch mobs were composed of people indoctrinated in the primary social institution of the region to conceive of African-Americans as extra-legal, extra-democratic objects, without rights which White person were required to respect. The indoctrination into the hierarchy of southern race relation was also facilitated by bringing White children to the occasion of a lynching and allowing them to view the bleeding and or burning corpses of African-Americans (Raper 1933). Largely, lynching was an institution maintained by prominent White people of the South to support the ruling class (Cox 1945). Interestingly, Cox (1945) noted that it would be foolhardy for African-Americans to seek the protection of the police, sheriff, or courthouse because that would further infuriate the lynch mob because of the assumption that the African-American was seeking to use the law to safeguard their rights which is antithetical to the lynchers' objectives. Lynching was quite effective in serving the purpose of keeping African-Americans in their place as an easily exploitable

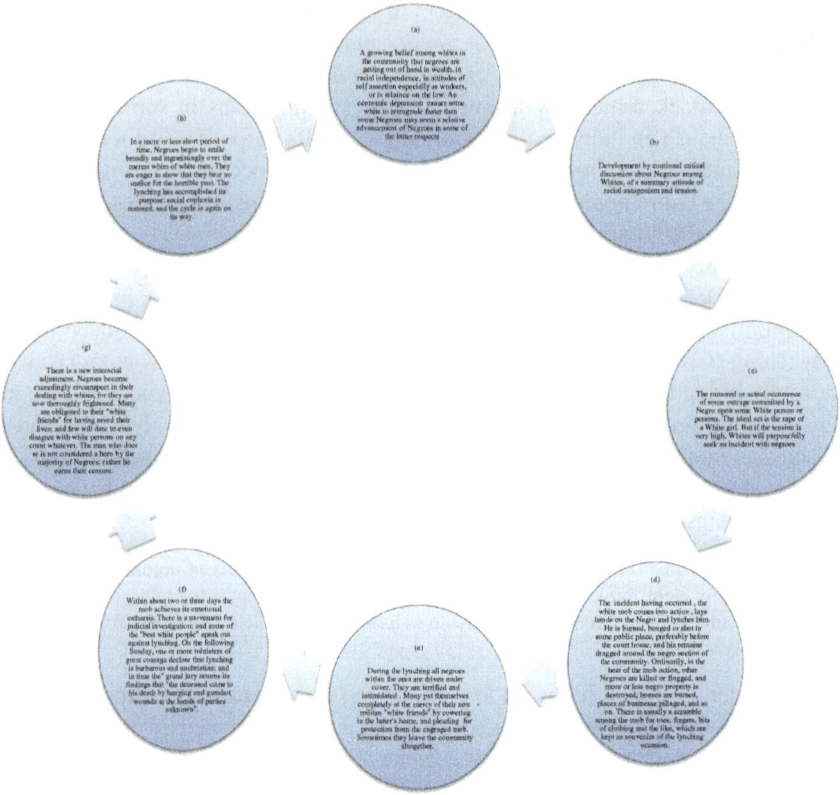

Fig. 1 The Lynching Cycle, *Source* Cox (1945: p. 576) Lynching and the status quo. Reproduced with permission of the Journal of Negro Education, copyright, 1945; Howard university

common labor reservoir (Cox 1945). Figure 1 illustrates the purpose and cycle of lynching as depicted by (Cox 1945).

However, victims of lynching were not always African-American. Other historically victimized groups by contemporary hate crime standards including Latinos, Native Americans, and Asian Americans were also lynched (Gonzales-Day 2006). Delgado (2009: p. 299) noted that "Mexicans were also lynched primarily in Arizona, California, New Mexico, and Texas, for like African-Americans, acting uppity, taking away jobs, making advances toward a white woman… with one exception, Mexican were lynched for acting to "Mexican"—"speaking Spanish' or defiantly reminding Anglos of their Mexicanness." Delgado (2009) noted the prevalence of lynching Latinos during and just after reconstruction was comparable to the rate of lynching African-Americans. To this point, Carrigan and Webb (2003) found that more than 400 Latino/Mexicans were lynched between 1848 and 1890.

Between 1882 and 1968, 4743 people were lynched of which the majority was African-American (Jacobs and Potter 1998). Between the years 1889 and 1918, the five most active lynching states were Mississippi (350), Louisiana (264), Texas (263), and Alabama (244) and these numbers include only recorded lynching (Jacobs and Potter 1998). The exact number of lynching is probably severely underestimated. To this point, Perlmutter (1992) asserted "Lynching was so common it was impossible to keep accurate records" (p. 151). Still, according to Cutler (1969), African-American lynching was so prevalent in the southern states that African-American lynching victim rates exceeded Whites by 350 %. Raper (1933) reported that between 1889 and 1932, there were 3745 reports of people lynched, of which 2954 were African-Americans and 791 were White persons.

The Chicago Tribune reported that between 1882 and 1903, a total of 3337 African-Americans were lynched by White mobs (Cutler 1969). Lynching of African-Americans was so prevalent during this period that, in a single year, 1892, a total of 200 African-Americans were lynched (Jacobs and Potter 1998). Lastly, the Equal Justice Initiative released a report in 2015 on lynching in America. Focusing primarily on lynching in southern states between 1877 and 1950, they identified 3959 people who were lynched including 700 that were previously unknown and what they describe as "terror lynching".

Although these numbers are disparate and underlie the lack of specificity regarding prevalence of lynching, they confirm the practice of lynching as the origins of contemporary hate crimes. Moreover, the practice of lynching denotes the mindset of the perpetrators similar to hate offenders today. Lynching victims, primarily African-Americans were not worthy or of equal standing to require due process of law in the form of trial. The humanity of African-Americans was not considered equivalent to White persons to require the ethical consideration of basic human rights afforded to persons. To a large extent, lynching served comparable purposes that are quite similar to the objectives of hate offenders detected in contemporary hate crimes.

It is important to note that lynching proliferated in the South just after President Abraham Lincoln signed the emancipation proclamation and the Thirteenth amendment was enacted. History indicates African-American Lynching was a response to the federal government efforts to remove legal constraints on African-American participation in America's social, legal, and economic systems. History also reveals evidence of the increasing prevalence of lynching during times when African-Americans were perceived to have succeeded socially and economically at the expense of Whites. Lynching historically and hate crimes contemporarily is a message of terror, intimidation and an effective reminder of past atrocities to direct and vicarious victims alike and larger society for victims to staying in their place of inferiority.

Ida B. Wells, the avowed anti-lynching journalist, noted that John Hughes of Missouri, Isaac Lincoln of South Carolina and Will Lewis of Tennessee was lynched for the serious charge of being "saucy" to White people (Wells-Barnett 1969). Brundage (1997: p. 2) noted lynching was a "powerful tool of intimidation" used by the White population to subordinate and subjugate the Black population. Similarly, King et al. (2009: p. 292) noted "lynching was perhaps the most egregious expression of overt prejudice and demands for white supremacy during the Jim

Crow era" that also "depicts the state's failure to protect a racial minority group from violent extra-legal social control".

It is in this tradition, that hate crime continues today as message crimes to primary victims, secondary members of the victim's group and society at large. Lynching and the message of White Supremacy were never more evident than in the birth and rebirths of the Ku Klux Klan.

The Birth and Rebirth of the Ku Klux Klan

Recall that lynching was most prevalent during brief periods of African-American social and economic prosperity. History also reflects that the birth and numerous rebirths of the Ku Klux Klan (KKK) also coincided with these periods of African-American economic, social, and political progress. The Ku Klux Klan was formed during the reconstruction era only two years after the passage of the Emancipation Proclamation in 1863. Two years later, in 1865, the Thirteenth Amendment was enacted abolishing and proscribing slavery in the United States. During this post civil war reconstruction period, Klansmen in white hooded robes terrorized southern Blacks so much that Blacks went into semi-permanent hiding (Chalmers 1981). Although African-Americans were legally free and slavery outlawed, the KKK's singular purpose was to intimidate African-Americans into not accessing social, political, and economic rights afforded them as free men and women. Klan membership and activity peaked during the reconstruction era as anger toward the abolition of slavery was followed by equally divisive reconstruction amendments requiring equal protection under the law for all citizens (Thirteenth Amendment) and prohibiting Federal and State governments from denying a citizen the right to vote based on "race, color or previous condition of servitude" (Fifteenth Amendment). During this era, the Klan's reign of terror effectively dispirited African-Americans who were previously buoyed by the possibilities of equality pursuant to the reconstruction amendments. Chalmers (1981: 14) noted:

> Unless there were federal troops at hand, the safest thing for Negroes to do was to hide during period of Klan activity or after outbreaks of violence. It was reported that in some region of South Carolina, more than a majority of the Negroes slept in the woods during the Klan's active winter of 1870-1871.

Not unlike contemporary hate offenders, the KKK's purpose was to prevent de facto implementation of the thirteenth, fourteenth, and fifteenth amendments through physical violence and psychological terror (Chen 2000). On one such occasion, Swinney (1987) described a race riot in March of 1871 during the trial of three Blacks accused of making incendiary speeches. While most of the Blacks escaped to the woods, 20 to 30 Blacks were shot and killed, and the KKK took the three Blacks on trial from the courthouse and hanged them.

During the last century, the KKK experienced several rebirths and a philosophical renaissance. Sadly, these rebirths reflect the stability and popularity of the KKK as an organizational and ideological vehicle of hate against a number of minority groups. Interestingly, the KKK membership has alternately waned and increased consistent with sociopolitical and economic equality rights advances. Klan membership in the 1920s has been estimated at 4–5 million; however, in 1974 its membership was estimated at a low of 1100; still, in 1981 membership increased to 11,000. Finally, between 1988 and 1997 Klan membership was reported at 5000 official members (ADL 1988; Baudouin 1997).

Although Klan membership waned in the late twentieth century, a plethora of other extremist organizations has emerged with Klan type extremist agendas. These include Neo-Nazis, The Christian Identity, Skinheads, and anti-tax, anti-government groups dedicated to espousing and acting on hate ideologies (Levin 2001). Comparable to the broader appeal of the contemporary KKK agenda, these groups also target an increasing number of diverse victim groups including African-Americans, Jews, LGBTQ persons, and immigrants. Jacobs and Potter (1998) noted that after the overturning of Plessy v. Furguson (1896) with the U.S. Supreme Court Decision in Brown v. Board of Education (1954) violence against Blacks and Jews flared across the south with hundreds of homes, churches, and synagogues experiencing firebombing. Consistent with the history of spikes in violence and Klan activity during periods of African-American social and economic progress, African-American students who attended newly desegregated schools required National Guard protection from angry White mobs livid and prepared to react violently over the Brown v. Board of Education decision. The births and rebirths of the Ku Klux Klan and its progeny again reflects the deep roots of hate-motivated behavior particularly during period of economic downturns where White persons perceived themselves as less fortunate than African-Americans and other minorities. The births and rebirths of the KKK provide an interesting temporal trajectory of hate-motivated behaviors in America.

Anti-semitism and Holocaust Denial

Next to the 400-year enslavement of African-Americans, perhaps the most notorious evidence of hate-motivated conduct in modern history is reflected in the genocide against Jewish people (Gerstenfeld 2013: p. 188). Some historians and scholars have described the genocidal victimization of Jewish people as the greatest holocaust in the history of civilization. Thus, the infamous name "The Holocaust" aptly describes the systematic extermination of approximately 6 million Jews between the years 1942 and 1945. Historical evidence inclusive of orders, documents, and testimonial evidence of the genocide were provided to interrogators at the Nuremberg trials in 1946. Levin (2001) noted that during the trials, defendants did not deny the genocide, but claimed they were obeying orders. Rudolf Hoess' testified in 1946 that he "personally arranged on orders received from Himmler in

May, 1941, the gassing of two million persons between June–July 1941 at the end of 1943, during which time I was Commandant of Auschwitz" (Stern 1003: p. 69).

Further, evidence of the holocaust estimates that, nearly 6 million Jews were asphyxiated, gassed, shot or used as anatomical subjects for human experiments throughout 17 concentration camps located throughout Eastern Europe. Often, those who were too young, weak or old, or unable to work in forced labor camps were immediately segregated and promptly sent to the concentration camps described as the most efficient killing machines in world history (Levin 2001). Those victims who could work, after a period of forced labor, were rounded up, stripped and herded in large enclosures where they knowingly awaited death from the administration of the insecticide zyklon b or carbon monoxide (Berenbaum 1993; Obrien and Palmer 1993).

Despite the physical and testimonial evidence, anti-Semitism reflected by the denial of the holocaust continues and has been revived nearly six decades after the end of the World War II. The Anti-Defamation League (ADL) describes holocaust denial as part of anti-Semitic propaganda movement active in the United States, Canada, and Western Europe that seeks to refute the evidence of the Nazi regime's systematic mass murder of 6 million Jews during World War II (www.adl.org). The ADL explains that holocaust denial, otherwise known as holocaust revisionism, is a propaganda campaign to rewrite history that has origins at the end of the World War II when it was apparent that Germany would lose the war (Lipstadt 1993). Lipstadt (1993) noted in her research on holocaust denial, that Heinrich Himmler, the infamous Third Reich leader, attempted to cover up the atrocities by instructing his camp commandants to destroy records, crematoria, and other signs of mass destruction of human beings. However, evidence of his 1943 speech at Pozman to his SS Generals directing that the mass murder of the Jews should be secreted and never recorded was found. Moreover, in 1945, fearful of testimonial evidence by Jews, Himmler signed an official order directing that the concentration camps never be surrendered and no prisoner should be allowed to fall into the hands of the enemies alive. This order remains a part of the physical evidence and historical record of the holocaust today. Himmler's unsuccessful attempt to conceal and cover up the genocide was his clear understanding and acknowledgement that the Nazi policy of hate and extermination as the final solution to the "Jewish Problem" would never be justified in the court of world opinion. Therefore, his veiled attempt to erase the record of "crimes against humanity" and eliminate witnesses was perhaps the first of overt and covert acts to deny the holocaust.

After the war, Nazi SS leaders who escaped immigrated to other parts of the world to ideal relocation venues where holocaust denial could thrive. Almost immediately, former Nazis began to employ their adept skills of propaganda to deny the holocaust and rewrite history (Stern 1993: p. 6). Friedrich Meinecke (1950) authored one of the early holocaust denial publications entitled "The German Catastrophe" which essentially attempted to neutralize the blame on Germany suggesting it was the work of industrialist and Semites. In addition, Frenchman former internee and avowed anti-Semite, Paul Rassinier was one of the most significant contributors to early holocaust denial propaganda. Rassinier's concentration camp experience as an internee at Buchenwald, the very first Nazi concentration camp, gave his voice and written word a veneer of credibility with contemporary holocaust deniers. However, Lipstadt (1993) pointed out that Buchenwald, Germany was only one of 17 concentration camps that happened to not have a gas chamber. Consequently, Rassinier's view is less credible and his claim "I was there and did not see a gas chamber" is discredited because he was not at any of the other 16 concentration camps.

Still, in 1948, just a few years after the war, Rassinier's (1948) published "Le Passage de la Ligne". Two years later, in 1950, he published "The Holocaust Story and the Lie of Ulysses". Both publications claimed the holocaust did not happen. A decade and a half later, Rassinier (1964) published "The Drama Of European Jewry" wherein he attempted to discredit what he called "the genocide myth". Rassinier authored numerous holocaust denial publications over the next three decades but these three are still employed by contemporary anti-Semitic holocaust deniers with two recurrent themes: denial of the existence of the gas chambers and the number of Jews who died.

Perhaps more detrimental, Rassinier's voice and written word continues today to suggest that holocaust allegations are a fabrication of a Jewish/Soviet/Allied conspiracy to swindle Germany out of billions of dollars in reparation. More importantly, Rassinier's (1978, 1978a) publications and his rationale of disingenuous benefactors of the holocaust hoax are still embraced by anti-Semites primarily in France but also in the United States.

It is important to note that the freedoms protected by the constitution in the United States also offer fertile ground for anti-Semitism in the form of holocaust denial. The United States with its staunch First Amendment purists and protectors of free speech also tangentially allow holocaust revisionism to grow unfettered in a manner proscribed by statutes in many European countries. Consequently, holocaust denial, unlike many countries in Europe and in Canada flourished and delivered quite effectively the message of anti-Semitism.[1]

American holocaust deniers operating under the protection of the First Amendment are empowered to proclaim Rassinier's recurring denial themes and the rationale of disingenuous reparation benefactors of a holocaust hoax. Nearly 50 years later, these themes are still embraced and reverberate in the hate philosophies of many extremist hate groups and want to be holocaust deniers.

Levin (2001) enumerated a number of factors that converged to give holocaust denial new life in a modern day denial philosophies embraced by an assortment of extremist groups. First, he explained that the evidence of the holocaust was so overwhelming and accepted throughout mainstream academia, theologians, and mass media, it became necessary for denial promoters to diversify their message to other extremist groups. Consequently, the shrinking KKK was willing to work with neo-Nazis against their common enemies. Levin (2001: p. 192) posited:

[1]Both Germany and Canada employ statutes that proscribe holocaust denial and race rhetoric likely to result in violence.

"The younger new, "Nazified" Klan did not share it previous leaders' distrust of neo-Nazis and were thus more susceptible to the denial message". In addition, the first generation 1950 and 1960s KKK lost it appeal and membership to a growing number of extremist splinter groups. Though African-American remained the targets of disdain, Jewish and anti-government conspiracy theories were now at the center of hate-related extremism. The leaders of these new groups such as Tom Metzer and David Duke and Richard Kelly Hoskins promoted their own extremist versions of holocaust denial (Levin 2001).

How does holocaust denial link to hate crimes? First, it is important to note that anti-Semitism as a specific type of bias constitutes the majority of the annually reported federal bias category of religion. Moreover, anti-Semitism is the one ubiquitous characteristic of all holocaust deniers that binds them together. Attack upon the truth under the guise of scholarship is an attempt to justify anti-Semitic viewpoints promoted by Nazis. Holocaust denial the foundation for modern day hate mongers to sustain their anti-Semitic beliefs, expand their ideologies and increase the likelihood of transferring these beliefs into hate crime conduct. The deep roots of hate lie firmly in European and American history and again on a trajectory that leads to contemporary hate crimes.

Gay and Lesbian Bashing

Homophobia or sexual prejudice (Herek 2000a) has a history as long as racism and anti-Semitism but not nearly as well documented (Gerstenfeld 2013). In fact, for most of the twentieth century, the stigmatization of homosexuality was taken for granted and largely unquestioned (Herek and Capitanio 1999; Herek 2000a). Homosexual persons were, and arguably still are, harassed and subjected to disdainful prejudice by offenders. Moreover, official policies and public sentiment reflected by law enforcement agencies sanctioned harassment of gay persons during the regular course of law and order maintenance in the first half of the twentieth century. It is in this historical context that homosexual persons today are subjected to the highest rate of violent victimizations. Worse, violence against homosexuals has been found to reflect the most heinous and physically injurious hate crime victimizations (Berrill 1990; Herek et al. 2002).

However, nearly 46 years ago, gay and lesbian persons grew tired of the mistreatment and harassment and made their voices of opposition heard. The Stonewall Inn rebellion sparked the modern day Gay Liberation Movement. That day, on June 28, 1969 at 1:20 AM in the morning eight New York City police officers (NYPD) raided the Stonewall Inn, a bar in New York's West Village frequented by gays and lesbian persons. The raid, typical of previous raids of the Stonewall Inn, was characteristic of the regular, tolerated, city-sanctioned harassment of gay persons by NYPD. Typically, upon entry into the bar, lights were turned on, music stopped and police officers proceeded to check customer conduct customer IDs. Employees, managers and patrons without ID or those patrons dressed in full drag[2] were immediately arrested. In 1969, it was illegal to serve gay persons alcohol or for gays to dance with one another.

However, unlike previous raids, gay and lesbian persons refused to cooperate with the police. Those who were asked to leave the bar congregated outside. As those persons who were the subjects of arrests complained of mistreatment, other patrons vociferously objected and loudly proclaimed allegations of harassment. Consequently, the eight officers decided to arrest all 200 patrons of the bar. While awaiting the patrol wagon, the perceived injustice caused a crowd of over 600 sympathizers outside to swell outside the bar. The angry crowd began to throw things at the police and forcing the eight police to barricade themselves inside the Stonewall Inn and await backup help from additional police officers. After numerous arrests and injuries to police and protesters, peace prevailed but the modern day gay and lesbian liberation rights movement was launched. Today the protest by the gay community at the Stonewall Inn is considered the Rosa Parks moment of the Gay Liberation Movement. No longer would gay and lesbian person just tolerate injustice and harassment. The launch of gay liberation movement became synonymous with gay pride, characterized by the rainbow flag proclaiming to all that the negative stereotype of homosexuality was no longer acceptable. In fact, one of the major victories of the gay rights movement was to eliminate diagnoses of homosexuality as a mental disorder in the Diagnostic and Statistical Manual[3] (Herek 2000a). Another victory credited to gay and lesbian activist is the radical change from treating homosexuality as a mental disorder to treating anti-gay hostility as a disorder. Herek (2000a) noted this was crystalized in the term "homophobia" coined originally by George Weinberg. Weinberg (1972) defined homophobia as the dread of being in close quarters with a homosexual or for homosexual themselves, self-loathing.

However, even with the social and political progress made through the advocacy of gay and lesbian activism since the Stonewall rebellion, hate crimes directed towards homosexual persons are still quite prevalent. Prejudice towards gay and lesbian person is endemic throughout mainstream America. A number of studies between 1984 and 1989 of various sample sizes, characteristics, and research methodologies found that harassment and violence against gay persons was quite pervasive (Berrill 1990). These studies generally lacked systematic data collection. However, almost 30 years after the launch of the gay and lesbian rights movement, Herek (2000b), found that 54 % of American felt that homosexual behavior is always wrong. Additionally, 44 % of Americans surveyed considered homosexuality an unacceptable life style. Franklin's (2000) study found that 10 % of high school and college students admitted to physical assault or threat to a homosexual. Moreover, 95 % reported witnessing verbal or physical abuse by friends. In a comprehensive study by National Gay and Lesbian Taskforce (1991) a sample of 2074 gay and lesbian male subjects from major cities in the United States including

[2]Denotes Men wearing women's clothing or women wearing Men's clothing.

[3]Prior to the DSM IV, homosexuality met the criteria as a mental disorder.

Boston, New York, Atlanta, St. Louis, Denver, Dallas, Los Angeles, and Seattle were surveyed. The study found that 19 % of the gay victims had been punched, kicked or beaten at least once in their lives because of their sex orientation. Forty-four percent had been threatened with physical violence and 94 % experienced verbal abuse, physical assault, police abuse, weapon assault, vandalism, and or being spat on. Eighty-four percent knew of other gays who had been victimized and 92 % experienced anti-gay epithets more than once. In addition, anti-gay violence had a major impact on the attitudes and future behavior of those surveyed. Eighty-three percent of those surveyed thought they would be victimized in the future and 62 % feared for their safety.

It should be noted that LGBT official hate crime victimization rates are likely underestimated because of fear of retaliation, public disclosure of the sex orientation, or secondary victimizations by police (Herek et al. 2002). Therefore, estimates of anti-gay violence are most likely conservative and not representative of the dark figure of LGBT victimizations. However, reports by advocacy groups and law enforcement agencies do suggest a growing trend in anti-gay violence (Berill 1990; Herek 1989; Herek et al. 1999, Herek et al. 2002; Dunbar 2006). In 2010, Klanwatch of the SPLC (2010) analyzed 14 years of FBI hate crime data to assess hate crime prevalence rates of minority groups most victimized by violent hate crimes. Using a computation method that compared each minority groups' percentage of violent victimizations to their percentage in the population, they found that gay persons were most victimized at 8.3 times the expected rate of victimization. Comparatively, Jews, Blacks, Muslims, and Latinos were victimized at 3.5, 3.2, 1.9, and 0.6 times, respectively, the expected rate of victimization. Further, when they compared gay violence victimization rates to other minority groups, gay persons were 2.4 times for likely to suffer a violent attack than Jews; 2.6 times more likely than Blacks; 4.4 times more likely than Muslims and 13.8 times more likely than Latinos[4] (www.splc.org).

In a subsequent study conducted by the Human Rights Campaign (2012), disparate relative rates of violent victimization of gay persons were reported. They found that LGBT youth were twice as likely as their straight peers to be verbally harassed or physically attacked. Moreover, a significant increase in prevalence anti-gay and Lesbian hate crimes was recently reported by the 2012 UCR report. Other studies have found that anti-gay violence appears particularly heinous and physical injuries are more severe than comparable nonbias crimes or bias crimes against other minorities (Herek et al. 1999; Millers and Humphrey 1980; Pezzella and Fetzer 2015). Millers and Humphrey (1980) studied homosexual victims of assault and murder and reported:

> An intense rage is present in nearly all homicide cases of gay victims. A striking feature… is their gruesome, often vicious nature. Seldom is the homosexual victim simply shot. He is more apt to be stabbed a dozen or more times, mutilated and strangled. (p. 179)

[4]Figures for Latino victimization rates do not include undocumented immigrants who fear reporting because of the possibility of deportation. Therefore the figures are less reliable.

So what explains the sustained prevalence and severity of anti-gay violence throughout American history? Several factors including the institutionalization of anti-gay ideology, social acceptance of anti-gay prejudice, and societal backlash to political and social gains achieved by the Gay and Lesbian liberation movement may explain the continuity of anti-gay violence. Gerstenfeld (2013) asserted that the institutionalization of anti-gay ideology is reflected by the actions and policies of several mainstream staples in American society. First, within the institution of politics, conservative anti-gay politicians and nonpolitical public figures openly voice their opposition to homosexuality under the guise of advocating mainstream traditional American values. In addition, religious institutions espousing anti-gay religious views on moral grounds have also adopted anti-gay political agendas. For instance, in 1996, Congress enacted the Defense of Marriage Act that authorized states to refuse to recognize same sex marriages from other states. In 2000, California passed a constitutional amendment authorizing the state to exclusively recognize only marriages between men and women. Other states have followed suit and only 11 states have enacted same sex marriage legislation via representatives from their respective states legislatures or by popular vote. Today, same sex marriage is legal in 37 states. However, 26 states derived legal authority via court decisions. Thirteen states still have constitutional amendments or state laws banning same sex marriages of which seven have had the bans overturned with appeals in progress. The U.S. military represents another major American institution that legitimated anti-gay bias and bigotry. To this point, just 4 years ago, the U.S. military sustained and enforced their "Don't Ask, Don't Tell" policy regarding sex orientation in the military which was eventually repealed by President Barack Obama in 2011.

In summary, victim accounts of historic eras of hate-motivated prevalence reflects the legacy of hate violence that is firmly entrenched in American History. Undoubtedly, historical evidence of other eras and episodes of hate exists that also serve to remind us of the historic and deepest antipathy that man has toward fellow man. Without recognizing the legacy associated with intergroup group animus, how can we devise effective policies that diminishes hate-motivated violence?

References

ADL. (1988). Hate Groups in America: A Record of Bigotry and Violence.

Baudouin, R. (1997). *The Ku Klux Klan: A History of Racism and Violence* (5th ed.). Montgomery, Al: Southern Poverty Law center.

Berenbaum, M., US Holocaust Memorial Museum. (1993). *The world must know: The history of the Holocaust as told in the United States Holocaust Museum*. Little, Brown.

Berrill, K. T. (1990). Anti-gay Violence and victimization in the United States an overview. *Journal of Interpersonal Violence, 5*(3), 274–294.

Brown v. Board of Education, U.S. Supreme Court 347 U.S. 483 (1954).

Brundage, W. F. (Ed.). (1997). *Under sentence of death: Lynching in the South*. UNC Press Books.

Carrigan, W. D., & Webb, C. (2003). The lynchings of persons of Mexican origin and descent in the U.S. 1848-1929. *Journal of Social History, 37*, 411–438.

Chalmers, D. M. (1981). *Hooded Americanism: The history of the Ku Klux Klan*. Duke University Press.

Chen, T. Y. L. (2000). Hate Violence as Border Patrol: An Asian American Theory of Hate Violence. *Asian LJ, 7*, 69.

Cox, Oliver. (1945). Lynching and the status quo. *Journal of Negro Education, 14*, 576–588.

Cutler, J. E. (1969). *Lynch-law. An investigation in the history of lynching in the United States*. Chicago: Negro Universities Press.

Delgado, R. (2009). The law of the noose: A history of Latino lynching. *Harvard Civil Rights-Civil Liberties Law Review, 44*, 297–312.

Dunbar, E. (2006). Race, gender, and sexual orientation in hate crime victimization: Identity politics or identity risks? *Violence & Victims, 3*(21), 323–337.

Equal Justice Initiative. (2015). Lynching in America: Confronting the legacy of racial terror. Montgomery, Al: Author. Retrieved from http://www.eji.org.

Franklin, K. (2000). Antigay behaviors among young adults: Prevalence, patterns, and motivators in a non-criminal population. *Journal of Interpersonal Violence, 15*, 339–362.

Gabbidon, S., & Greene, H. (2016). *Race & Crime*. 4th edition Sage.

Gerstenfeld, P. B. (2013). *Hate crimes: Causes, controls, and controversies*. Sage.

Gonzales-Day, K. (2006). *Lynching in the West, 1850–1935*. Duke University Press.

Herek, G. M. (1989). Hate crimes against lesbians and gay men: Issues for research and policy. *American Psychologist, 44*(6), 948.

Herek, G. M. (2000a). The psychology of sexual prejudice. *Current directions in psychological science, 9*(1), 19–22.

Herek, G. M. (2000b). Sexual prejudice and gender: Do heterosexual attitudes towards lesbian and gay men differ? *Journal of Social Issues, 56*(2), 252–266.

Herek, G. M., & Capitanio, J. P. (1999). AIDS stigma and sexual prejudice. *American Behavioral Scientist, 42*(7), 1130–1147.

Herek, G. M., Gillis, J. R., & Cogan, J. C. (1999). Psychological sequelae of hate-crime victimization among lesbian, gay, and bisexual adults. *Journal of Consulting and Clinical Psychology, 67*(6), 945.

Herek, G. M., Cogan, J. C., & Gillis, J. R. (2002). Victim experiences in hate crimes based on sexual orientation. *Journal of Social Issues, 58*(2), 319–339.

Howard, W. (2005). *Lynchings: Extralegal violence in Florida during the 1930s*. iUniverse.

Human Rights Campaign. (2012). *Growing Up LGBT in America*. Key Findings: HRC Youth Survey report.

Jacobs, J. B., & Potter, K. (1998). *Hate crimes: Criminal law & identity politics* (Vol. 67). New York: Oxford University Press.

King, R. D., Messner, S. F., & Baller, R. D. (2009). Contemporary hate crimes, law enforcement, and the legacy of racial violence. *American Sociological Review, 74*(2), 291–315.

Levin, B. (2001). History as a Weapon: How Extremists Deny the Holocaust in North America. *American Behavioral Scientist, 44*(6), 1001–1031.

Lipstadt, D. E. (1993). *Denying the Holocaust: The growing assault on truth and memory*. Simon and Schuster.

Meinecke, F. (1950). *The German Catastrophe, (transl. SB Fay)*. Cambridge, Mass.

Miller, B., & Humphreys, L. (1980). Lifestyles and Violence: Homosexual victims of assault and murder. *Qualitative Sociology, 3*(3), 169–185.

National Gay and Lesbian Taskforce. (1991). *AntiGay/Lesbian Violence, Victimization, and Defamation in 1990*. National Gay and Lesbian Taskforce Policy Institute: Washington D.C.

Obrien, J., & Palmer, M. (1993). *The state of region atlas*. New York: Simon & Schuster.

Perlmutter, P. (1992). *Divided we fall. A history of ethnic, religious, and racial prejudice in America*. Ames: Iowa State University press.

Petrosino, C. (1999). Connecting the past to the future hate crime in America. *Journal of Contemporary Criminal Justice, 15*(1), 22–47.

Pezzella, F. S., & Fetzer, M. D. (2015). The likelihood of injury among bias crimes: An analysis of general and specific bias types. *Journal of Interpersonal Violence*, 0886260515586374.

Plessy v. Furguson, U.S. Supreme Court 163 U.S. 527 (1896).

Raper, A. (1933). *The Tragedy of Lynching*. Reprint, Montclair, NJ: Patterson Smith. (1969).

Rassinier, P. (1978a). *Debunking the Genocide Myth* (pp. 1939–1945). Torrance: Institute for Historical Review.

Rassinier, P. (1978). *The Holocaust story and the lies of Ulysses: a study of the German concentration camps and the alleged extermination of European Jewry*. Inst for Historical Review.

Stern, K. S. (1993). *Holocaust denial*. New york: American Jewish Committee.

Swinney, E. (1987). *Suppressing the Ku Klux Klan: The enforcement of reconstruction amendments 1870–1877*. Dissertation-G.

The Anti-Gay Lobby: The Family Research council, the American Family Association & the Demonization of LGBT People, The Math: Anti-LGBT Violence retrieved from http://www.splc.org.

Wells-Barnett, I. B. (1969). On lynchings: Southern horrors [1892], A red record [1895], Mob rule in New Orleans [1900].

Weinberg, G. H. (1972). *Society and the healthy homosexual*. Macmillan.

www.adl.org.

Chapter 3
The Case for Hate Crime Statutes-Putative Uniqueness of Injuries

Hate crime statutes are primarily based on the notion that hate-motivated criminal behavior is more injurious than parallel non-hate-motivated offenses (Iganski 2002; Herek et al. 2002; Lawrence 2009; Perry 2009; Pezzella and Fetzer 2015). Moreover, proponents of hate crime statutes argue that hate crimes are message crimes sent to vicarious victims who possess similar immutable characteristics and group membership as the primary victim. Perhaps the most significant evidence of the uniqueness of hate crimes is the multidimensional injuries primary and vicarious victims sustain. The multidimensional impact of hate crimes include a plethora of physical, psychological, emotional and behavioral injuries to the victim. As a result, the elevated severity of harm characterized by the multidimensional nature of hate crime injuries is reflected in penalty enhancement or substantive criminal law statutes that upgrade punishment beyond that of parallel non-hate-motivated crimes.

Proponents of hate crime statutes argue several justifications for treating hate-motivated offenders more severely than their ordinary crime counterparts. First, they contend hate crime statutes that enhance penalties provide for protection of primary victims of the hate attack and vicarious victims inclusive of all members of the primary bias victim's group. Levin (2002) posited that hate crimes are serial in nature and extend the initial victimization to subsequent and secondary victimizations. As a result, Levin (2002) argued governments have a compelling interest in precluding justification for retaliatory victimizations. Concern for retaliatory victimization was also mentioned in the Wisconsin V. Mitchell, U.S. 505 U.S. 476 (1993) decision, wherein the Court noted "hate crimes are thought to be more likely to provoke retaliatory crimes, inflict distinct emotional harm on their victims, and incite community unrest." Acknowledging the capacity of hate crimes to incite retaliatory victimization and community unrest, the Oregon Court of Appeals also posited that hate crimes have "the power to escalate from individual conflicts to mass disturbances" (State v. Beebe, 67 Or. App. 738 1994). The issue of retaliatory victimizations was also delineated in the legislative findings supporting the enactment of 18 U.S. 249, the Matthew Shepard and Robert Byrd Jr. Hate Crime Prevention Act:

© The Author(s) 2017

F.S. Pezzella, *Hate Crime Statutes*, SpringerBriefs in Policing,
DOI 10.1007/978-3-319-40842-2_3

> A prominent characteristic of violent crime motivated by bias is that it devastates not just the actual victim and the family and friends of the victim, but frequently savages the community sharing traits that caused the victim to be selected.

In addition to primary, serial, and secondary victimizations, proponents of hate crime statutes argue that hate crimes are more psychologically and physically injurious than their ordinary crime counterparts (Levin and McDevitt 1993; Boeckman and Petrosino 2002; Messner et al. 2004; Lim 2009; Perry 2014; Iganski and Lagou 2014; Pezzella and Fetzer 2015).

Psychological Injuries

Hate scholars posit that the psychological trauma of hate crimes exist in the aftermath of the hate crime incident. Several studies incorporating varying methodologies and samples have found hate victims sustain elevated rates of fear and emotional trauma directly related to their victimization. Berrill's (1990) study of antigay violence and victimization surveys in the United States reported gay and lesbian men not only fear antigay harassment and violence, but also anticipate victimizations in the future. Specifically, between 51 and 79 % feared for their safety and between 76 and 88 % expected to be future targets of antigay violence. Barnes and Ephross (1994) used a small sample of 59 bias victims to compare bias and non-bias victimizations and found the most prevalent reaction of bias victims was anger followed by fear. In a national telephone victimization survey of over 2000 respondents, Erlich et al. (1994) compared victimization experiences in four groups of non-victims, group defamation victims, personal crime victims, and bias victims. Bias crime victims reflected the greatest number of psychophysiological symptoms of post-traumatic stress and social and behavioral changes. The report concluded that hate crime victims suffered through major life changing patterns and were significantly more nervous, lost more friends, incurred more insomnia, and generally found themselves unable to concentrate.

Herek et al. (1999) conducted one of the most comprehensive studies of the deleterious effects of hate crime victimizations on gay and lesbian persons. Incorporating a convenience sample of 2000 gay, lesbian and bisexual respondents, they found distinct adverse psychological sequelae associated with gay and lesbian victimizations up to 5 years after the incident. Gay and lesbian victims of bias crimes relative to non-bias victims, experienced excessive levels of depressive symptoms, crime related anxiety, anger, and slower rates of recovery. In later research, Herek et al. (2002) interviewed another convenience sample of 450 lesbian and gay victims and again detected higher levels of fear and psychological stress in bias victims relative to non-victims during the same period.

McDevitt et al. (2001) conducted another comprehensive study of the psychological and behavioral aftermath of bias victimizations. They utilized a sample of bias and non-bias assaults victims using victim agency advocate and Boston police records from 1992–1997. Although the study retained low victim response rates to their survey instrument, numerous psychological, behavioral, and situational factors distinguished bias from non-bias victimizations. Bias victims cited that they were more nervous, depressed, sustained trouble concentrating, thought about the incident longer, and felt like they didn't wish to live any longer much more than their non-bias victims counterparts. Moreover, bias victims were less likely to feel safe after the incident, more likely to incur health problems, and a divorce or separation or loss of employment. McDevitt et al. (2001) concluded that bias victims had more difficulty coping after the victimization and appear to have additional problems with their recovery process due to their prolonged fear and more intrusive thoughts. Further, they noted this finding supported the earlier hypothesis of victim interchangeability. Victim Interchangeability in the mindset of primary or potential secondary victims means "any individual who possesses or perceived to possess, a specific trait could be selected as a target" (McDevitt et al. 2001: p. 698). McDevitt et al. (2001) and other hate scholars (Lim 2009; Perry 2001, 2009, 2014) posit that victim interchangeability adds another level of psychological trauma to the victimization experience primarily because of the victim's inability to reconcile control of potential future hate attacks through some physical change in their behavior scholars conceptualize as victim blaming. Victim blaming is an internal psychological process that allows victims to recall their own decisions prior to the victimization and then to consider alternate and changeable ways of avoiding future victimization. However, because hate victims are chosen exactly because of immutable characteristics interchangeable with any in their groups, victim blaming is not in the psychological repertoire of most hate crime victims. Consequently, because victims are interchangeable, they are unable to proactively do anything to escape their chances of future victimization by changing their sense of vulnerability.

In a cross-sectional study of 350 lesbian, gay, and bisexual (LGB) youths, Dragowski et al. (2011) examined the relationship between significant life experiences of sex orientation LGB victims and post-traumatic stress symptoms (PSS). They found that verbal and physical sexual orientation victimizations, childhood gender, atypicality, and internalized homophobia were all individually related to post-traumatic stress. Verbal and physical sexual orientation victimization explained PSS over all the study's other variables. Internalized homophobia, stressful life events, and verbal sexual orientation victimization were found to be the most significant predictors of PSS among LGB youth.

Finally, in a study incorporating the most representative and hence, generalizable sample, Iganski and Lagou (2014) analyzed a 6 years sample of multidimensional injuries reported by victims from the British Crime survey. A comparison of physical, emotional, psychological, and behavioral injuries between bias and non-bias victims were assessed in their analyses. They found that Bias crime victims reported they were "more likely to have an emotional reaction to the incident and with greater intensity compared with otherwise motivated crimes" (p. 41). Moreover, they found the gap between the two groups widened when the extent of the emotional reaction was considered. "Victims in incidents of hate crimes were over twice as likely as victims in incidents of otherwise motivated crimes to state that they had been affected very much" (p. 41).

Physical Injuries

Hate crime statute advocates also posit that bias crimes are physically more injurious and brutal than parallel non-bias crimes. Levin's (1999) analysis of hate crime assaults found that that they were twice as likely to cause injury and four times more likely to require hospitalization. Levine and McDevitt's (1993) review of 452 Boston police hate crime records detected that 50 % of the hate crime cases resulted in severe physical injury requiring hospitalization. They noted the excessively brutal nature of bias crime cases. Similarly, Strom (2001) analyzed aggravated assaults derived from the 1997 through 1999 National Incident-Based Reporting system (NIBRS). He found that sixty percent of the total bias crimes studied involved serious injuries to victims. Messner et al. (2004) used a 1999 NIBRS sample to analyze intimidation, simple, and aggravated assaults. They found that race and other biases were almost three times more likely to result in major injuries including broken bones, severe lacerations, etc. compared to non-bias cases. In a recent study of assaults incorporating a 2010 NIBRS sample, Pezzella and Fetzer (2015) found that anti-white and lesbian victims sustained the most severe injuries in comparison to other bias types.

However, other research on the severity of physical injuries did not detect differences between bias and non-bias crimes. A few studies found non-bias crimes more likely to sustain severe injuries. Martin (1996) analyzed comparable cases of assaults from New York City and Baltimore County bias crime units and found that non-bias (49 %) exceeded bias (27 %) injuries in Baltimore County. Similarly, non-bias (93 %) exceeded bias (81 %) injuries in New York City. McDevitt et al. (2001) found similar results in their study of injuries. They reported an association between the extent of medical treatment received by respondents and type of victimization. Non-bias victims (52.1 %) who received emergency medical services or hospital treatment reflected a statistically significant higher rate of hospitalization than bias victims (37.1 %). Iganski and Lagou (2014) assessment of victimization experiences found that hate-motivated victims were less likely to report injuries than to report no injuries unlike victims of non-bias motivated crimes who were more likely to report injuries compared to reporting no injuries. Studies of the physical injuries of hate crimes have produced mixed results.

Secondary Victimization Effects

The vicarious and deleterious effect of hate crimes on proximal and distal victims has also been studied (Weinstein 1992; Perry 2001, 2014; Perry and Alvi 2012; Iganski and Lagou 2014). Weinstein (1992) posited that race violence inflicts an "in terrorem effect: an intimidation of the group by the victimization of one or more members of that group" and to society at large. Perry and Alvi (2012) analyzed "in terrorem" victimization effects in their analysis of secondary victimizations derived from focus group discussions and analysis of a nonprobability sample of vicarious victims. They reported secondary victim "in terrorem" effects inclusive of feelings of shock, anger, fear/vulnerability, inferiority, and normativity on vicarious victims. They posited that secondary victims realize that another group wishes to exert power; reinforce inferiority and subordination; and force acceptance that hate crimes, stigmatization and marginalization is normative within our society.

Not unlike international terrorism, recall the goal of the hate crime attack is to send a message of superiority, vulnerability, and imminent danger to victims (Lim 2009; Perry and Alvi 2012). According to Lim (2009) and Perry and Alvi (2012) the hate message is often received with the full effect of the offender's intention. The sense of victim interchangeability causes vicarious victims that are proximally and distally close to the primary victim to sense the constant threat of violence. Consequently, vicarious victims change and safeguard their behavior while unconsciously accepting bias victimization as normative possibility consistent with the threat of victim interchangeability. Thus, a proximal effect of hate crimes is the stigmatization of group members and the developing sense of vulnerability to potential future victimization as normative. Under these dire circumstances, feelings of safety and security for vicarious victims slowly erode (Levin and McDevitt 1993; Lim 2009; Perry 2014). According to Lim's (2009) content analysis, Asian American secondary victims fear for their safety and livelihood when aware of a hate crime attack against another Asian American. Consequently, hate violence permeates the minds of secondary victims and is anticipated and firmly managed through constrained choices of how far to depart from the group members' ecological comfort zone.

Perhaps the most distal victim of bias motivated behaviors is society as a whole (Weinstein 1992; Iganski 2001; Perry 2014). Violence motivated by hate affirms natural intergroup suspicion, creates separation, and undermines the possibility of intergroup collective efficacy (Perry 2014). Perry (2014) refers to this as the collateral damage impact on shared values. She notes that hate crimes, if left unchallenged, will deteriorate relationships between communities and long deeply held values of inclusion, equity, and justice. Voluntary segregation, or the exercise of restricting one's self to the immediate community to avoid repeat victimization is a natural reaction to hate-motivated violence. Unfortunately, this is also compliant with the offender's purpose to intimidate and compel subordinate behavior.

In summary, proponents of hate crime statutes argue hate crimes uniquely injure primary and secondary victims and society at large. Empirical evidence is mixed regarding the distinct severity of hate crimes injuries; however, both theoretical and empirical findings suggest hate crimes inflict emotional and behavioral injuries. The most distal victim of hate crimes is society itself when democratic ideals of inclusion and collective efficacy are undermined and the potential for intergroup distrust and conflict is escalated.

References

Barnes, A., & Ephross, P. H. (1994). The impact of hate violence on victims: Emotional and behavioral responses to attacks. *Social Work, 39*(3), 247–251.

Berrill, K. T. (1990). Anti-gay violence and victimization in the United States an overview. *Journal of Interpersonal Violence, 5*(3), 274–294.

Boeckmann, R. J., & Turpin-Petrosino, C. (2002). Understanding the harm of hate crime. *Journal of Social Issues, 58*(2), 207–225.

Dragowski, E. A., Kalkitis, P. N., Grossman, A. H., & D'Augelli, A. R. (2011). Sexual orientation victimization and post traumatic stress symptoms among lesbian, gay, and bisexual youth. *Jornal of Gay and Lesbian Social Services, 23*(2), 226–249.

Erlich, H., Larcom, B., & Pervis, R. (1994). *The traumatic effects of ethnoviolence*. Towson, Md: Prejudice Institute, Center for the Applied Study of Ethnoviolence.

Herek, G. M., Gillis, J. R., & Cogan, J. C. (1999). Psychological sequelae of hate-crime victimization among lesbian, gay, and bisexual adults. *Journal of Consulting and Clinical Psychology, 67*(6), 945.

Herek, G. M., Cogan, J. C., & Gillis, J. R. (2002). Victim experiences in hate crimes based on sexual orientation. *Journal of Social Issues, 58*(2), 319–339.

Iganski, P. (2001). Hate crimes hurt more. *American Behavioral Scientist, 45*(4), 626–638.

Iganski, P. (2002). Introduction: The problem of hate crimes and hate crimes laws. In P. Iganski (Ed.), *The hate debate: Should hate be punished as a crime*. (pp. 1–15). London: The Institute for Jewish Policy Research.

Iganski, P., & Lagou, S. (2014). The personal injuries of 'hate crime'. In *The Routledge international handbook on hate crime*, pp. 34–46.

Lawrence, F. M. (2009). *Punishing hate: Bias crimes under American law*. Harvard University Press.

Levin, B. (1999). Hate crimes worse by definition. *Journal of Contemporary Criminal Justice, 15*(1), 6–21.

Levin, Brian. (2002). From slavery to hate crime laws: The emergence of race and status-based protection in American criminal law. *Journal of Social Issues, 58*(2), 227–245.

Levin, J., & McDevitt, J. (1993). *Hate crimes: The rising tide of bigotry and bloodshed* (Vol. 5). New York: Plenum Press.

Lim, H. A. (2009). Beyond the immediate victim: Understanding hate crimes as message crimes. *Hate crimes: The consequences of hate crime, 2*, 107–222.

Martin, S. E. (1996). Investigating hate crimes: Case characteristics and law enforcement responses. *Justice Quarterly, 13*(3), 455–480.

McDevitt, J., Balboni, J., Garcia, L., & Gu, J. (2001). Consequences for victims: A comparison of bias and non-bias motivated assaults. *American Behavioral Scientist, 45*, 697–713.

Messner, S. F., McHugh, S., & Felson, R. B. (2004). Distinctive characteristics of assaults motivated by bias. *Criminology, 42*(3), 585–618.

Perry, B. (2001). *In the name of hate: Understanding hate crimes*. Psychology Press.

Perry, B. (Ed.). (2009). *Hate crimes* (Vol. 2). Greenwood Publishing Group.

Perry, B. (2014). Exploring the community impacts of hate crimes. In *The Routledge international handbook on hate crime*.

Perry, B., & Alvi, S. (2012). 'We are all vulnerable' The in terrorem effects of hate crimes. *International Review of Victimology, 18*(1), 57–71.

Pezzella, F. S., & Fetzer, M. D. (2015). The likelihood of injury among bias crimes: An analysis of general and specific bias types. *Journal of Interpersonal Violence*, 0886260515586374.

State v. Beebe. (1994). 67 Or. App. 738.

Strom, K. (2001). *Hate crimes reported in NIBRS, 1997–99*. US Department of Justice, Office of Justice Programs, Bureau of Justice Statistics.

The Matthew Shepard & Robert Byrd Jr. Hate Crime Prevention Act 18 U.S. 249.

Weinstein, J. (1992). First amendment challenges to hate crime legislation: Where's the speech?.

Wisconsin V. Mitchell. (1993). U.S. Supreme Court, 505 U.S. 476.

Chapter 4
Offenders, Victims, and Situational Characteristics of the Hate Crime Incident

An understanding of the motive and characteristics of offenders and the nature of harm to the victim is vital to the assessment of the hate crime incident. In this respect, it is important to note the social, demographic characteristics of both offenders and victims and the situational circumstances surrounding hate crime incidents. Incident details inclusive of the date, time, and place of the hate crime incident may conceivably provide insight into precipitators of hate crimes and illuminate cues that trigger hate crime incidents. (Wortley 2001). To examine these issues, analyses of studies of hate crimes that have incorporated the UCR, NIBRS, and NCVS are assessed to present a demographic and situational context for understanding hate crime offending.

Offender Characteristics

The United States Department of Justice 2012 Hate Crime Statistics Report (2014) reflected 5331 known offenders where at least an attribute of the offender was identified. Of these known offenders, 54.6 % were White and 23.3 % were Black. Of the 5790 single bias incidents, the bias category of race accounted for 2797 (48 %) of all the incidents. A deeper analysis into the bias category of race reveals that the bias victimization type, anti-Black, accounted for 805 (65 %) of all race bias incidents in 2012. A total of 1771 (63 %) of the 2822 known race bias offenders were White. The bias type, anti-White accounted for 657 (23 %) of all race bias incidents. A total of 756 (26 %) of race bias offenders were black. The bias category of religion accounted for 1099 (19 %) of all single bias incidents of which 674 (61 %) were anti-Semitic hate crime incidents. A little less than half, 232 (48 %) of the 484 religious bias category of offenders were anti-Semitic offenders. The 2012 UCR reports typical ages of offenders were 17 and under (32 %), 18–24 (29 %), and 25–34 (17 %).

Utilizing NIBRS, Strom (2001) provided an insightful report of victimization experiences perpetrated by offenders for the three years period between 1997–1999.

© The Author(s) 2017

F.S. Pezzella, *Hate Crime Statutes*, SpringerBriefs in Policing,
DOI 10.1007/978-3-319-40842-2_4

The majority of persons suspected of committing hate crimes were White males consistent with later NIBRS and NCVS analyses (Messner et al. 2004; Harlow 2005; Langton and Planty 2011; Wilson 2014; Pezzella and Fetzer 2015). Strom (2001) also found that among those suspected of violent hate crimes, 60 % were white males, 21 % were black males, and 10 % white females. This finding is consistent with Wilson's NCVS assessment of victim perception of hate crime offenders. Wilson (2014) reported that in 2011 victims perceived the most prevalent violent hate crime offender was White (58 %); followed by Black (24 %). However, in 2012, victim perception of violent hate crime offenders changed: White offenders (34 %) followed by Black offenders (32 %) and other race offenders (17 %) comprised the most prevalent characteristics perceived by victims as the most violent hate crime offenders.[1]

Strom (2001) found that White offenders also represented the most prevalent property related hate crime offenses. A total of 69 % of property offenders were White males and 15 % were White females. Assessing hate crimes by bias motivation Strom (2001) also found that White offenders were the most prevalent offenders comprising 88 % of religious bias crimes; 85 % of disability bias crimes; 84 % of sex orientation bias crimes; 82 % of ethnic bias crimes, and 66 % of racial bias crimes. With respect to ages of offenders, Strom (2001) found that the age 17 and under comprised 33 % of all offenders; age 18–24 comprised 29 %; ages 25–34 constituted 17 % of all bias offenses. The age distribution is consistent with Freilich and Chermak's (2013) report in problem oriented policing (pop) guide number 72 that half of all hate offenders are under the age of 20.

Interestingly, Messner et al. (2004) and Pezzella and Fetzer (2015) analyses of NIBRS found the age group of offenders between 16 and 25 more likely to exact a severe injury to their victims. The findings from these NIBRS studies vary from Freilich and Chermak's (2013) pop guide that violent hate crime offenders tend to be older than property crime offenders. Strom (2001) also found that offenders under the age of 18 comprise a sizable proportion of arrestees for simple assault, 29 % and intimidation, (33 %) and damage, destruction or vandalism of property, 66 %. Moreover, 75 % of arrestees were white; 85 % were male including 66 % White males; 18 %, Black males, and 1 % other race males.

The NCVS findings of offender characteristics are quite noteworthy in light of the representative data sampling techniques utilized in the survey of victims. Because of access to victims, the NCVS taps into the elusive dark figure of hate crime victimizations unavailable in UCR and NIBRS data. Incorporating NCVS data, Wilson's (2014) analysis of demographic characteristics of violent hate offenders found that males accounted for 66 and 61 % offenses in 2004 and 2012, respectively. Moreover, in 2012, White, Black, and other races comprised (34, 32 and 17 %) of race characteristics of hate offenders. Wilson's (2014) NCVS victimization analysis also reflected variation from the UCR and NIBRS reports of the

[1]Wilson found in 2004 Black offenders (41 %) comprised the most prevalent violent hate crime offenders followed by White offenders (30 %) and other races (17 %).

typical ages of offenders. The NCVS report indicated that the ages of hate crime offenders are increasing. In 2004, victim estimates of offender ages were 17 and under (28 %); 18–29 (20 %); and 30 and older (24 %). However, by 2012, victims estimates of offenders ages were modified: 17 and under (19 %); 18–29 (13 %); and 30 and older (41 %). Wilson (2014) also reported a substantial change in victim perception of the most prevalent offender bias category from ethnic bias from 2004 (22 %) to 2012 (51 %) constituting a 29 % increase over the 9 years period. Concurrently, victim's perception offenders' race bias diminished by 12 % from 2004 (58 %) to 2012 (46 %). Other bias offender prevalence rates in 2012 were as follows: victim association with people having certain characteristics (34 %); religion, (28 %); and gender bias, (26 %). Moreover, while perceived ethnic bias more than doubled, perceived religious bias nearly tripled from (10 %) in 2004 to 28 % in 2012.

Victim Characteristics

Victim characteristics and prevalence rates reflect a similar disparity observed for offender characteristics rates derived from the analyses of the 2012 UCR, and the NIBRS and the NCVS studies. The 2012 UCR reported 7164 victims comprised of anti-Black victims 2295, (32 %); anti-White victims, 763 (11 %); anti-Jewish victims 836, (12 %); anti-male homosexual victims 754 (11 %), and anti-Hispanic 393 (5 %). These victim characteristics are inconsistent with Strom's (2001) NIBRS analyses. Strom (2001) found (40 %) of all hate crime victims between 1997 and 1999 were White males; White females (25 %); Black males (20 %), and Black females (12 %). Strom's findings also vary from later NIBRS analyses. Messner et al. (2004) found that compared to no bias motivation, Black and males victims were more likely to be the target of a bias motivated crime. Similarly, Pezzella and Fetzer (2015) found that the odds of an assaultive offense being biased increased by 67 and 75 % when the victim was Black and male compared to when the victim was White and female.

However, several special victimization reports support Strom's findings. Harlow (2005) found that per 1000 persons, White victims (0.9), Hispanic victims (0.9), and Black victims (0.7) reflected the rank order of most prevalent characteristic of hate crime victims. Similarly, Langton and Planty (2011) special report on victimization found that White (61 %) Hispanic (17 %) and Black (13 %) victims retained the same rank order of the most prevalent victim characteristics. Wilson's (2014) later report victimization found a comparable rank order of victim characteristics with White (52 %), Hispanic (30 %), and Black (13 %) victims constituting the most prevalent characteristics of violent hate crime victims. Recall, Wilson (2014) reported the Hispanic victimization rate doubled over the previous 9 years.

With regard to sex and age of victims, almost all the studies of victims indicate that males are most likely to be victims. Messner et al. (2004) and Pezzella and Fetzer (2015) found the age group between 16 and 25 not significantly different than ages over 25 regarding the likelihood of experiencing a bias victimization. However, descriptive analyses of Strom (2001) and several victimization studies dispute these findings. Strom (2001) found age categories of victims almost evenly distributed: 13–17 (17 %); 18–24 (21 %); 25–34 (21 %); and 35–44 (19 %). Harlow (2005) reported the ages 17 and under, 18–20, 21–29, and 30 or older comprised 19.75, 6.5, 21.4, and 38.1 %, respectively as the percent of victims of crimes of violence. Wilson (2014) comparison of victimization trends over nine years detected variation in the rate of victimization by race and age. In 2004, male and White victims comprised 60 and 74 % of violent hate crime victims, respectively while Black/African American and Hispanic/Latino constituted less than 4 and 17 % of violent hate victimizations, respectively. However Wilson (2014) found the age category between 12–17 (33 %) comprised the most violently victimized age category. Next were, 18–24 (20 %), 25–34 (14 %), and 35–49 (23 %). The NCVS analysis also indicated that hate crime victimizations are inversely related to household income. In 2004, violent victim household income categories of $24,999 or less (33 %); $25,000–$49,000, (23 %) and 50,000 or more, (26 %) reflected the distribution of victims by household income.

In 2012, rates of victimization by sex, race, and age changed. Male and White offenders accounted for 53 and 52 % of victims. Age categories of victims varied a little with a major reduction in the victimization of 12–17 year olds (24 %); 18–24 year olds (23 %); 25–34 year old (11 %); 35–49 (20 %) and a spike in victimization of victims between 50 and 64 from 8 % in 2004 to 21 % in 2012. During the period household income of victims fluctuated as well with income of 24,999 or less (32 %); 25,000–49,999 (15 %); and $50,000 or more (37 %).

Situational Characteristics of the Hate Crime Incident

An analysis of NIBRS used in tandem with the NCVS allows a view into the situational circumstances surrounding hate crime incidents. Strom (2001) reported the most frequent of location of bias incidents occur at a residence (32 %); and then by open space, (28 %) and finally, commercial and retail enterprises (19 %). However, the choice of venue for hate victimizations may be more nuanced; peak prevalence rates for race (31 %) and ethnicity (34 %) occurred in open space. By contrast, 41% of sex orientation crimes occurred in a residence and 23% occurred in open space.

The other NIBRS studies detected similar findings. Messner et al. (2004) and Pezzella and Fetzer (2015) found that males and Blacks were more likely to be victimized by hate-motivated aggravated assault. Both NIBRS studies found that bias assaults were more likely to occur outside the home and involve strangers. Moreover, they confirmed earlier findings that African-Americans were at highest risk of becoming victims of racially motivated bias. In addition, theses studies confirm that bias incidents are more likely when alcohol and drugs are present (Messner et al. 2004; Freilich and Chermak 2013; Pezzella and Fetzer 2015).

The analysis of injuries in Messner et al. (2004) and Pezzella and Fetzer (2015) NIBRS studies indicated bias crimes are not significantly different than nonbias crimes with respect to the severity of injury to victims. However, the likelihood of injury of a bias crime victim was found to be higher: when a stranger was involved; when three or more offenders were involved; when a weapon was involved; or when the incident happened on the street. Wilson's (2014) NCVS report also confirmed previous findings of insignificant differences in severity of injuries between bias and nonbias offenses. In 2012, the NCVS reported that a 20 % injury prevalence rate for violent hate crime victimizations. However, there was no statistically significant difference in 2012 between the percentage of violent hate (20 %) and violent non-hate (24 %) crime victimizations in which the victim sustained an injury.

Assessing weapon use, Strom (2001) noted that 70 % of aggravated assaults involved a weapon in the incident; of those 17 % was for a firearm; 17 % for a knife or sharp object; 19 % for a blunt object; and 16 % for any vehicle or any other weapon. Similarly, Messner et al. (2004) and Pezzella and Fetzer (2015) found the use of firearms, knives, and blunt objects when compared to no weapons in a bias incident more likely to result in serious injury. Wilson's (2014) victimization study reported weapons were also found in 24 % of the violent hate crime victimizations in 2012; however, no statistically significant difference was reported between the percentage of violent hate (24 %) and violent non-hate (20 %) crime victimizations in which the offender was known to have a weapon. The absence of significant differences in comparative prevalence rates between bias and nonbias crimes on the use of weapons and the severity of injury is noteworthy. These findings suggest that although ethnic bias and subsequently race bias may be the most prevalent bias categories, they are as likely to incur a weapon or injury related bias victimization as any nonbias victimization. Freilich and Chermak (2013) pop guide number 72 reinforced the situational characteristics detected in these studies:

> The offenders are more likely to be under the influence of drugs or alcohol and more likely to seriously injure victims when compared to offenders who commit other types of assaults. Compared to regular crimes, hate offenses are more likely to involve strangers, multiple offenders, and victims, and occur in public places (p. 6).

A few studies have also reported the dates and times when hate crimes are more than likely to occur. Spikes in hate crimes often occur around local, national, and international events such as 9/11 and or special dates such as Adolph Hitler's birthday (Freilich and Chermak 2013). The time of day hate crime incidents occur also seems somewhat nuanced. Strom (2001) found that two-thirds of victims age 17 and under were more likely to be victimized during the day between 7 a.m. and 6 p.m. However, violent hate crime involving victims age 18–24 were more likely to occur in the late evening with a peak around midnight with a quarter of the violent incidents occurring between 10 p.m. and 1 a.m. However, Harlow's (2005) victimization study reported violent hate crimes occur most frequently between noon and 6 p.m. (42.5 %), followed by 6 p.m. to midnight (29 %), 6 a.m. to noon (18.7 %), and midnight to 6 a.m. (7.9 %).

Bias Crime Offender Typology

Delineating offender and victim bias incident prevalence rates and situational factors relevant to the bias incident provides an invaluable context with which to assess the spatial and temporal dimensions of the hate crime. Still, insight into hate offenders' mindset can also be determined by the nature of hate offense. To this end, McDevitt et al. (2002) study of 358 Boston Community Disorder Unit hate crime cases established the basis for expanding the 1993 typology of hate crime offenders. Thus, the typology was augmented to add the 2002 finding of retaliatory hate offenders to the thrill seeking, defensive and mission hate crime offenders that comprised the original typology. Although quite dated, the typology continues to describe the variety of bias motivation categories of offenders most likely to commit hate crimes (Gerstenfeld 2013).

The Thrill Seeking Offender

McDevitt et al. (2002) posited the thrill seeking hate offender represents nearly 2/3 of all hate motivated crime offenders. The motivating force for the thrill-seeking hate offender is the thrill itself especially in the absence of any other stimulus. The thrill seeking hate offender does not necessarily have a specified animus toward the victim of his hate incident but will often follow others who do. They generally lack conviction for their bias motivated crime but rarely do they refuse to go along for fear of rejection by their friends or to attain bragging rights (Gerstenfeld 2013).

For example, Byers and Crider (2002) conducted interviews with eight young men who were accused of hate-motivated offenses against Amish victims. Among other reasons, offenders reported that generating excitement and eliminating boredom was a common explanation by offenders for their behavior. Others reported they were going along with friends and did not want to back out. Similarly, Franklin (2000) surveyed 489 college students about their attitudes and behaviors toward gays and lesbians. They found that 10 % actually threatened or physically assaulted people they perceived to be homosexual; another 23 % admitted to verbal harassment. Four factors were reported to account for offender motivations. These included peer dynamic reflecting the desire to please peers, antigay ideology, thrill seeking and self-defense. Both peer dynamics and thrill seeking factors easily coincide under Levin and McDevitt's (1993) thrill-seeking model. Interestingly, McDevitt et al. (2002) noted that in 91 % of the cases in their study, the offender left their own neighborhood and sought a victim elsewhere such as a gay pride parade, a synagogue, or a minority neighborhood.

Messner et al. (2004) explained that bias offenders were just as likely as other offenders to act impulsively; moreover, they posited that hate crime was more of a reflection of criminality than hatred for a group. Citing support for Gottfredson and Hirschi's (1990) general theory of crime, they posited the similarities between bias and nonbias crimes diminished the role of bigotry as a motivation for selection of the hate victim; rather they argued that hate offenders are as impetuous as conventional offenders and therefore share the same propensity for criminality irrespective of any particular bias motivation. Recall, Messner et al. (2004) also contend that alcohol and drug use, in conjunction with general criminality underlie most unprovoked and random brutal bias attacks. They argued that the random motive and nature of these hate crime incident was evidence of a thrill-seeking generalist bias offender in lieu of a focused hate-motivated offender. Interestingly, they found that these otherwise non-motivated thrill seeking bias offenders sustained a greater likelihood of facilitating a violent incident and other anti-social behaviors and consequently, severe physical injuries to victims.

The Defensive Bias Offender

The defensive bias offender reflects a different motivating force underlying the bias incident. The defensive bias offender perceives himself as the protector of a valued tangible asset or intangible right. The defensive offender is generally not associated with an organized group; however, unlike the thrill seeking offender he directs his attack at a specific victim who reflects the perceived intrusion. Generally, there are incidents that trigger group expression of anger (Gerstenfeld 2013). The trigger in defensive hate crimes may vary from a loss in competition for housing, employment, or progressive social issues such as same sex marriage or interracial couples. Arguably, the aggravated assaults on African American anti-Trump for President protestors in Chicago in March, 2016 by otherwise nonviolent Trump supporters reflect the behavior of a defensive bias offenders.[2]

Levin and McDevitt (1993) noted that defensive hate crime offenders rarely leave their own neighborhood to seek out victims; victims just happen upon them. However, Levin and McDevitt (1993) noted there was often an economic theme to supplement the offenders' primary feelings of intrusion. To this point, Levin (2002) posited that increases in hate crime have paralleled increases in intergroup competition. Consequently, the burgeoning threat to historically advantaged groups since the early 1980s has inspired an increase in hate incidents (Levin and McDevitt 1993). Some researchers have found hate crimes prevalent in "defended" White neighborhoods that have experienced an in-migration of minorities (Green et al. 1998). However, Levin (2002) suggests dabblers in hate crimes may defend any aspect of their lives they feel especially entitled to hold: not only what they perceive as their neighborhood, but their campus, their dormitory, their office or their social relationships. Frequently, international conflicts are the catalyst for the occurrence of defensive hate crimes that can prompt peremptory strikes against perceived threat

---

[2]Donald Trumps campaign strategy was based on taking back America and the losses sustained by President Obama's catering to the interest and perceived gains of minority groups.

from outsiders. McDevitt et al. (2002) reported defensive hate crime offenders retain an inordinate belief in their own entitlement.

Mission Bias Offenders

Mission bias offenders commit the least prevalent of bias offenses but potentially the most lethal and violent of the four within the typology. Mission offenders harbor the animus for other groups that are not so clear in thrill-seeking and defensive bias offenders. In their view, all minority or marginalized groups are dangerous and wish to destroy the American culture, economy, and purity of racial heritage. Mission offenders perceive a higher order purpose from God to carry out their goal of eliminating an entire group of people. The perpetrator is typically a conspiratorial thinker but often he may suffer from mental illness that produces hallucinations, impaired, ability to reason, and withdrawal from other people (McDevitt et al. 2002). Mission offenders, unlike thrill seekers and defensive hate crime offenders, will never be satisfied with acts of vandalism and intimidation. He may rationalize the need for retribution for all the problems he has suffered. Moreover, in his paranoid delusions, he perceives a conspiracy against him for which he seeks revenge. Mission hate crime offenders primarily commit solo, random, but extreme acts of violence often on multiple unsuspecting victims with whom the offender has directed his wrath. Gerstenfeld (2013) posited that mission hate crimes though uncommon, deserve attention due to the extreme amount of violence involved and the psychological factors underlying the mission criminal's behavior. Ironically, The Matthew Shepard and Robert Byrd Jr. Hate Crime Prevention Act of 2009 was named after victims of two of the most heinous race and sex orientation bias crimes perpetrated by mission offenders. However, mission-driven bias motivated crimes are relatively infrequent compared to thrill seeking and defensive hate crimes. McDevitt and colleagues estimate less than 5 % of hate crimes may be mission-driven hate crimes.

The Retaliatory Bias Offender

The last in typology is the retaliatory bias offender. In McDevitt et al. (2002) study of bias motivations they found that 8 % of the offender motivations could be classified as retaliatory bias crimes. The retaliatory bias offender typically hears about a hate crime incident against his/her group and takes revenge by committing a hate crime against any member of the alleged initial group. Recall, the possibility of retaliatory bias incidents was mentioned as a congressional finding to support the enactment of Mathew Shepard and James Byrd Jr. Hate Crime Prevention Act (18 U.S. 249). The offenders perceive themselves as getting even for a hate crime committed against their group. Gerstenfeld (2013) posited that the Levin and

McDevitt (1993) typology of offenders has been used as a guide by law enforcement for investigating hate crime incidents and conceivably may be the most complex evidenced-based study of hate offender profiles available. However, although there is anecdotal research support for the typology (Franklin 2000; Byers and Crider 2002), the data from which the typology is derived is now more than 14 years old and from a single city. Consequently, bias research on offender motivations is somewhat dated. Moreover, some question the utility of the typology in assigning levels of culpability as their authors claim. To this point, Freilich and Chermak (2013) suggest another category of bias offenders. They posit that bias peripheral/mixed offenders are those offenders that commit hate crimes for mixed reasons, with hate appearing to be peripheral to the criminal incident. That is, the offenses may be only partly motivated by hate. Often, an otherwise non-hate motivated offense will escalate the dispute into a physical attack while using racial, religious, or ethnic slurs. Mixed bias motivated offenses are difficult for the police to classify and for prosecutors to prove hate motivated bias beyond a reasonable doubt. This issue is presented at length in Chap. 7 under the discussion of the dilemmas law enforcement and prosecutors encounter attempting to assess and prove bias motivation.

References

Byers, B. D., & Crider, B. W. (2002). Hate crimes against the Amish: A qualitative analysis of bias motivation using routine activities theory. *Deviant Behavior, 23*(2), 115–148.

Franklin, K. (2000). Antigay behaviors among young adults prevalence, patterns, and motivators in a noncriminal population. *Journal of interpersonal violence, 15*(4), 339–362.

Freilich, J. D., & Chermak, S. M. (2013). *Hate Crimes* (p. 72). Problem-oriented guides for police: Problem-Specific Guides Series.

Gerstenfeld, P. B. (2013). *Hate crimes: Causes, controls, and controversies*. Sage.

Gottfredson, M. R., & Hirschi, T. (1990). *A general theory of crime*. Stanford University Press.

Green, D. P., Glaser, J., & Rich, A. (1998). From lynching to gay bashing: The elusive connection between economic conditions and hate crime. *Journal of Personality and Social Psychology, 75*(1), 82.

Harlow, C. W. (2005). Hate Crimes Reported by Victims and Police. *Bureau of Justice Statistics Special Report*. Washington D.C.: U.S. Department of Justice, Bureau of Justice statistics.

Levin, B. (2002). From slavery to hate crime laws: The emergence of race and status-based protection in American criminal law. *Journal of Social Issues, 58*(2), 227–245.

Langton, L. & Planty, M., (2011). Hate crime, 2003–2009. *Special Report*. Washington D.C.: U.S. Department of Justice, Office of Justice Programs, Bureau of Justice statistics.

Levin, J., & McDevitt, J. (1993). *Hate crimes: The rising tide of bigotry and bloodshed* (Vol. 5). New York: Plenum Press.

McDevitt, J., Levin, J., & Bennett, S. (2002). Hate crime offenders: An expanded typology. *Journal of Social Issues, 58*(2), 303–317.

Messner, S. F., McHugh, S., & Felson, R. B. (2004). Distinctive characteristics of assaults motivated by bias. *Criminology, 42*(3), 585–618.

Pezzella, F. S., & Fetzer, M. D. (2015). The likelihood of injury among bias crimes: An analysis of general and specific bias types. *Journal of interpersonal violence*, 0886260515586374.

Strom, K. (2001). *Hate crimes reported in NIBRS, 1997–99*. US Department of Justice, Office of Justice Programs, Bureau of Justice Statistics.

United States Department of Justice, Federal Bureau of Investigation. (2014, December). *Hate Crime Statistics, 2012*. Retrieved 3 September 2015 from https://www.fbi.gov/about-us/cjis/ucr/hate-crime/2012/tables-and-data-declarations/1tabledatadecpdf/table_1_incidents_offenses_victims_and_known_offenders_by_bias_motivation_2012.xls.

Wilson, M. M. (2014). Bureau of Justice Statistics, US Dept. of Justice, Office of Justice Programs, United States of America. (2014). Hate crime victimization, 2004–2012.

Wortley, R. (2001). A classification of techniques for controlling situational precipitators of crime. *Security Journal, 14*(4), 63–82.

Chapter 5
Legislative Responses to Hate Crimes

The first hate crime statutes purposely designed to outlaw hate-motivated violence originated as a result of the victimization of Blacks during the reconstruction era of the United States. Essentially, congress enacted a series of civil rights statutes as a legislative response to burgeoning racial violence perpetrated against newly emancipated former slaves.[1] Recall, the Emancipation Proclamation and other legislation empowering former slaves with both freedom and citizen constitutional rights were also the catalyst for racial violence from outraged White southerners. During the post civil war era, the notion of guaranteeing civil rights to former slaves was antithetical to the thinking of many disenfranchised former White slave owners. Moreover, the precept of white racial superiority enabled the practice of slavery and the rationalization to perpetrate violence mostly through lynching to assure newly liberated slaves did not endeavor to exercise their new rights. Equally important, the precept of racial superiority essentially defined the social hierarchy between White and Black citizens that would permeate the next century of race based socialization practices. Just because the federal law recognized and legally empowered newly liberated Black citizens certainly did not mean a change in the cultural mores and practices of racial superiority (King et al. 2009). Therefore, contemporary hate crime statutes with origins just over 25 years ago are preceded

---

[1]These included the Emancipation Proclamation; the Civil Rights Acts of 1866 and 1871; the enactment of Fourteenth Amendment (1868); the ratification of the Fifteenth Amendment (1870); the Enforcement Acts (1870) (1871) and finally the Civil Rights Act of 1875. These federal legislative initiatives liberated former slaves; provided penalties for interference with the rights of Blacks either in concert or with others or in their capacity as government employees; provided for equal protection; the right to vote; and full and equal enjoyment to all citizens of public accommodations, places of public amusement and conveyances regardless of race, color or previous condition of servitude respectively. (The Civil Rights Act of 1875 was repealed.) Most of these provisions are presently codified under 18 U.S. § 241, 18 U.S. § 242, 18 U.S. § 245; and 42 U.S. §1983.

© The Author(s) 2017

F.S. Pezzella, *Hate Crime Statutes*, SpringerBriefs in Policing,
DOI 10.1007/978-3-319-40842-2_5

by congressional legislation enacted more than a century ago to address the identical issue of hate and race motivated violence (Swinney 1987).

Between the promulgation of the Hate Crime Statistics Act in 1990, and 2015, 46 states, the District of Columbia and federal government statutorily proscribe hate or bias crimes in a typology of sentencing enhancement, substantive aggravated offense, and data collection statutes (Franklin 2002; Gillis 2013; Pezzella and Fetzer 2015). These statutes are primarily drafted as racial animus, discriminatory selection, or "because of" or "by reason" of statutes.

Racial Animus, Discriminatory Selection, Because of, and Intent to Harass and Intimidate" Statutes

Hate crime statutes primarily increase the sentence or the severity of the offense when the bias-motivated conduct is determined. Penalty enhancement statutes based on discriminatory selection of protected victim groups have been found constitutional (Wisconsin v. Mitchell 1993). The Federal government and many states have enacted statutes with the broader less burdensome evidentiary requirement of discriminatory selection. However, other states have enacted statutes that require proof of racial animus beyond a reasonable doubt, posing a stringent burden on prosecutors (Barclay v. Florida 1983). For a significant number of states, culpability is determined by mere discriminatory selection of victims; in others, culpability is established by evidence of animus toward a "protected group" (Grattet and Jenness 2001; Lawrence 2002; Adams 2005; Dixon and Gadd 2014). While animus may be inferred from conduct stemming from discriminatory selection, the basis for blameworthiness represents a unique distinction in the rationale for enacting hate crime statutes. Hate crime statutes modeled under animus look to the reason for the discriminatory selection and proscribe criminal bias-motivated conduct because of prejudice and hostility toward the victim and the particular group he or she represents (Lawrence 2009; Grattet and Jenness 2001). Alternatively, animus statutes require that defendants have acted out of hatred for a specific group and the victim as a member of that specific group (Lawrence 2009). Moreover, they focus attention on the reason for discriminatory selection with the motivation for selection of primary importance. Motivation is less instrumental and more expressive in animus statutes (Grattet and Jenness 2001). "Because of" statutes are more stringent than discriminatory selection but less burdensome than animus statutes. Likewise "intent to harass and intimidate" statutes are less onorus than animus statutes but still require the prosecutor to establish the perpetrator had the state of mind to "intentionally harass and intimidate" the victim which can be difficult to prove. Grattet and Jenness (2001) notes that the "because of" or "intent to harass and intimidate" motivational phrasing has become the most popular wording in state statutes subsequent to 1990. Alternatively, discriminatory selection statutes do not distinguish the reason for selection. The entire basis of the statute is the discriminatory selection of the victim within a broad-based bias category. Discriminatory selection statutes incorporate the broader definition of hate crime simply requiring that victim selection be based on certain characteristics regardless of the perpetrator's ideology or hatred for a particular group. Discriminatory selection statutes are quite prevalent because of their administrative efficiency; the federal government incorporates the discriminatory selection model (Grattet and Jenness 2001; Pezzella and Fetzer 2015). The following federal and state hate crime statutes reflect the evolution of hate crime legislation in the U.S. Six state hate statutes are provided to illuminate the variation in groups protected under the legislation and to contrast differences in evidentiary criteria to establish bias motivation.

Title 28 U.S. § 534—The Hate Crime Statistics Act

The Hate Crime Statistics Act otherwise known as the HCSA of 1990 was the first hate crime legislation enacted after 18 U.S. § 245.[2] The HCSA of 1990 mandated the Attorney General collect data about hate crimes motivated by bias against a person's race, religion, disability, sexual orientation, or ethnicity. The bill also required the Attorney General to establish guidelines for the collection of the data including necessary evidence and criteria for a finding of manifest prejudice (Woods 2014).

Title 28 U.S. § 994—The Hate Crime Sentencing Enhancement Act of 1994

The HCSA did not include an enforcement provision. Enforcement provisions, however, were a significant jurisdictional expansion with the promulgation of Title 28 U.S. § 994, The Hate Crime Sentencing Enhancement Act (HCSE) of 1994 (otherwise known as the Violent Crime Control and Law Enforcement Act). The HCSE directed the US Sentencing Commission (USSC) to provide a sentence enhancement of "not less than three offense levels for offenses that the finder of fact at trial determines beyond a reasonable doubt are hate crimes." Further, the provision defined hate crimes as "a crime in which the defendant intentionally selected a victim, or in the case of a property crime, the property that is the object of the crime, because of the actual or perceived race, color, religion, national origin, ethnicity, gender, disability, or sexual orientation of any person." In 1995, the USSC implemented these guidelines to apply exclusively to federal crimes. This statute is the federal equivalent to many of the states' hate crime penalty

[2]18 U.S. § 245, often considered the first federal hate crime statutes was enacted in 1968 to protect citizens against interference from exercising federally protected activities.

enhancement statutes, applied, inter alia, to attacks and vandalism that occur in national parks and on other federal property.

Title 42 U.S. § 13701—The Violence Against Women Act of 1994

Congress also passed the Violence Against Women Act (VAWA) that provided that victims of gender based violence could sue their attackers and receive compensatory and punitive damages (Gerstenfeld 2013). The law provided authority for domestic violence and rape crisis centers and for education and training programs for law enforcement and prosecutors (ADL 2012). Under VAWA "All persons within the U.S. shall have the right to be free from crimes of violence motivated by gender." However, a portion of the VAWA was declared unconstitutional by the Supreme Court in 2000 because it exceeded congress' authority under the commerce clause.

Title 18 U.S. § 247—The Church Arson Prevention Act of 1996

The Church Arson Prevention Act was enacted after recognition of a reported spike in the church burnings that included predominantly African American congregations. According to the ADL (2012), it serves as a graphic reminder that America long struggle against racial and religious intolerance is far from over (p. 15). To this point, the Justice Department, opened 658 investigations of suspicious fires, bombings, and attempted bombings and made 225 arrest involving 301 suspects between January of 1995 and August of 1998 (ADL 2012). The law provided for facilitating federal prosecution and enhanced penalties for damaging places of worship (Gerstenfeld 2013).

Title 18 U.S. § 249 Matthew Shepard and James Byrd, Jr., Hate Crimes Prevention Act of 2009

The most recent of the federal hate crime statutes, 18 U.S. § 249 broadens federal authority and the number of protected groups by adding gender and gender identity and removing the jurisdictional requirement of a federally protected activity. This broadening of the Title 28 U.S. § 994—(The Hate Crime Sentencing Enhancement act of 1994) makes it unlawful to willfully cause bodily injury—or attempting to do so with fire, firearm, or other dangerous weapon—when 1), the crime was committed because of the actual or perceived race, color, religion, and national origin of any person, or 2), the crime was committed because of the actual or perceived religion, national origin, gender, sexual orientation, gender identity, or disability of any person and the crime affected interstate or foreign commerce or occurred within federal special maritime and territorial jurisdiction. This statute extended the number of bias types afforded hate crime "status" protection to include gender and gender identity. The law also provides funding and technical assistance to state, local, and tribal jurisdictions to help them to more effectively investigate, prosecute, and prevent hate crimes. Most importantly, the law expanded federal jurisdiction prescribed federal activities and thus empowered further empowered federal enforcement of hate crime laws. Punishment for violating this statute includes a maximum 10-year-prison term, unless death (or attempts to kill) results from the offense, or unless the offense includes kidnapping or attempted kidnapping, or aggravated sexual abuse or attempted aggravated sexual abuse. For offenses not resulting in death, there is a 7-year statute of limitations. For offenses resulting in death, there is no statute of limitations.

Select State Hate Crime Statutes

Code of Virginia 18.2-57 (1997): A mandatory prison term is required "if the person intentionally selects the person against whom (the crime is committed) because of his race, religious conviction, color or national origin."

Del. Code Ann. 1304: A person is guilty of a hate crime when he "selects the victim because of the victims race, religion, color, disability, national origin or ancestry."

La. Rev. Stat. Ann. Sec 14: **107.2**: It shall be unlawful for any person to select the victim of certain offenses against person and property because of actual or perceived race, gender, religion, color, creed, disability, sexual orientation, national origin, or ancestry of that person or the owner or occupant of that property or because of actual or perceived membership or service in, or employment with, an organization…. If the underlying offense is a misdemeanor and the victim is selected in the manner proscribed, then the offender may be fined no more than $500 or imprisoned for 6 months; If the underlying offense is a felony and the victim is selected in the manner proscribed, then the offender may be fined no more than $5000 or imprisoned with or without hard labor for 5 years or both. The sentences for either the misdemeanor or felony shall run consecutive to the underlying offense.

N.H. Rev. Stat. Ann. § 651:6 1F: A convicted person may be sentenced according to paragraph III if the jury also finds beyond a reasonable doubt that such person: 1(f) Was substantially motivated to commit the crime because of hostility toward the victim's religion, race, creed, sexual orientation as defined in RSA 21:49, national origin or sex.

Ohio Rev. Stat. Ann. § 2927.12: Ethnic Intimidation—No person shall violate Sect. 2903.21, 2903.22, 2909.06, or 2909.07, or division (A)(3), (4), or (5) of

Sect. 2917.21 of the Revised Code by reason of the race, color, religion, or national origin of another person or group of persons. (B) Whoever violates this section is guilty of ethnic intimidation. Ethnic intimidation is an offense of the next higher degree than the offense the commission of which is a necessary element of ethnic intimidation.

Vt. Stat. Ann. Tit. 13 s 1455: Imposes additional penalties on a person who commits, causes to be committed, or attempts to commit an crime and whose conduct is maliciously motivated by the victim's actual or perceived race, color, religion, national origin, sex, ancestry, age, and service in the armed forces of the U.S., handicap as defined by 21 V.S.A. sec 495d (5), sexual orientation or gender.

Contemporary hate crime legislation enacted in the last few decades clearly has a great deal more enforcement power than the original civil rights statutes. However, a cursory reading of the sample of federal and state statutes provided here, illustrates that the statutes vary substantially with respect to the victims groups designated for protection and the evidentiary criteria to establish bias motivation. For instance, the federal hate crime statute includes actual or perceived race, color, religion, national origin, gender, sexual orientation, gender identity, or disability of any person. In contrast, the Code of Virginia includes race, religious conviction, color, or national origin. The Delaware code adds disability and ancestry while the Louisiana hate crime statute includes actual or perceived race, gender, religion, color, creed, disability, sexual orientation, national origin, or ancestry of that person or the owner or occupant of that property or because of actual or perceived membership or service in, or employment with, an organization. Alternatively, the Ohio Ethnic Intimidation statute is less inclusive providing for enhanced penalties for those convicted of hate crime. Ohio incorporates an ethnic intimidation discriminatory selection statute that enhances penalty for ethnic intimidation when certain offenses are committed "by reason of" the victim's race, color, religion, or national origin. The Ohio statute does not includes sex orientation, gender or gender identity. Finally, the Vermont code adds age and service in the armed forces to the list of protected status groups.

This sample of federal and state statutes also illustrates the variation in evidentiary criteria. The Delaware, Virginia, and federal statutes are penalty enhancement type statutes that are based on discriminatory selection of victims. The New Hampshire and Vermont statutes require the more rigorous animus criteria to prove bias motivation. For instance, The New Hampshire statute increases penalties upon proof the defendant "was substantially motivated to commit the crime because of hostility toward the victim's religion, race, creed, sexual orientation." Alternatively, the Louisiana and Ohio statutes incorporate the "because of" motivational phrasing striking the middle ground between the administratively easy "discriminatory selection" and the stringent proof criteria of "animus." Contemporary hate crime statutes have expanded the number of protected groups and provided for severe sanctions. However, major constitutional and practical enforcement challenges plague the application of these statutes. Constitutional and policy issues surrounding these statutes are considered next.

References

Adams, D. M. (2005). Punishing hate and achieving equality. *Criminal Justice Ethics, 24*(1), 19–30.
ADL. (2012). Hate crime laws.
Barclay v. Florida. (1983). U.S. Supreme Court, 463 U.S. 939.
Code of Virginia. (1997). 18.2–57.
Del. Code Ann. 1304.
Dixon, B., & Gadd, D. (2014). Look before you leap: Hate crime legislation reconsidered. *South African Crime Quarterly, 40*, 25–30.
Franklin, K. (2002). Good intentions: The enforcement of hate crime penalty-enhancement statutes. *American Behavioral Scientist, 46*, 154–172.
Gerstenfeld, P. B. (2013). *Hate crimes: Causes, controls, and controversies*. Sage.
Gillis, B. (2013). Understanding hate crime statutes and building towards a better system in Texas. *American Journal of Criminal Law*.
Grattet, R., & Jenness, V. (2001). Examining the boundaries of hate crime law: Disabilities and the dilemma of difference. *Journal of Criminal Law and Criminology, 91*, 653.
King, R. D., Messner, S. F., & Baller, R. D. (2009). Contemporary hate crimes, law enforcement, and the legacy of racial violence. *American Sociological Review, 74*(2), 291–315.
La. Rev. Stat. Ann. 14: §107.2.
Lawrence, F. M. (2002). Racial violence on a 'small island': Bias crime in a multicultural society. *The Hate Debate. Should Hate be Punished as a Crime*.
Lawrence, F. M. (2009). *Punishing hate: Bias crimes under American law*. Harvard University Press.
N.H. Rev. Stat. Ann. § 651:6 1F.
Ohio Rev. Stat. Ann. § 2927.12.
Pezzella, F. S., & Fetzer, M. D. (2015). The likelihood of injury among bias crimes: An analysis of general and specific bias types. *Journal of Interpersonal Violence*, 0886260515586374.
Swinney, E. (1987). Suppressing the Ku Klux Klan: The enforcement of reconstruction amendments 1870–1877 Dissertation-G.
Title 18 U.S. § 247—The Church Arson Prevention Act of 1996.
Title 18 U.S. § 249 Matthew Shepard and James Byrd, Jr., Hate Crimes Prevention Act of 2009.
Title 28 U.S. § 534—The Hate Crime Statistics Act of 1990.
Title 28 U.S. § 994—The Hate Crime Sentencing Enhancement Act of 1994.
Title 42 § 13701—The Violence Against Women Act of 1994.
Vt. Stat. Ann. Tit. 13 § 1455.
Wisconsin v. Mitchell. (1993). U.S. Supreme Court, 505 U.S. 476.
Woods, J. B. (2014). Hate crime in the United States. In N. Hall, A. Corp, P. Giannasi & J. Grieve (Eds.), *International handbook on hate crime*. UK: Routledge.

Chapter 6
Constitutional and Public Policy Issues

In the early 1990s, two significant Supreme Court cases generated a plethora of constitutional and policy issues associated with hate crime legislation. The Courts in RAV v. City of St. Paul Minnesota 505 U.S. 377 and Wisconsin v. Mitchell 508 U.S. 476 reaffirmed the importance of content neutral statutes and the authority of the states to enact penalty enhancement discriminatory selection statutes, respectively. Thereafter, amidst controversy, most states and the federal government enacted hate crime statutes.

RAV v. City of St. Paul 505 U.S. 377 (1992)

In *RAV v. City of St. Paul* 505 U.S. 377 (1992), the defendant was convicted of violating the City of St. Paul, Minnesota hate crime ordinance by evidence that the defendant placed a burning cross on an African-American person's lawn. After granting certiorari, the U.S. Supreme Court struck down the City of St. Paul Bias crime ordinance, asserting that it was impermissibly content-based and thus violated the defendant's First Amendment rights. The Court ruled "the ordinance proscribed fighting words of whatever manner that communicate messages of racial, gender, or religious tolerance. Selectivity of this sort creates the possibility that the city is seeking to handicap the expression of particular ideas." The Court asserted: "the only interest distinctively served by the content limitation is that of displaying the city council's special hostility toward the particular biases thus singled out. That is what the first amendment forbids." The Court distinguished protected symbolic expression from unprotected conduct under the First Amendment. Moreover, the Court ruled content biased legislation proscribing disfavored forms of expression unconstitutionally violated the First Amendment requirement of statutory content neutrality. However, a year later, in Wisconsin v. Mitchell, 508 U.S. 476 (1993), the Court ruled statutes proscribing discriminatory selection conduct and enhanced penalties were permissible.

© The Author(s) 2017

F.S. Pezzella, *Hate Crime Statutes*, SpringerBriefs in Policing,
DOI 10.1007/978-3-319-40842-2_6

Wisconsin v. Mitchell 508 U.S. 476 (1993)

The U.S. Supreme Court in *Wisconsin v. Mitchell* 508 U.S. 476 unanimously upheld the constitutionality of the Wisconsin hate crime penalty enhancement statute that provided for an enhanced sentence where the defendant "intentionally selects the person against whom the crime is committed because of race, religion, color, disability, sexual orientation, national origin or ancestry of that person." The defendant in Mitchell had incited a group of Black men who had just finish watching the movie "Mississippi Burning" to assault a young White man by asking, "Do you all feel hyped up to move on some white people," and by calling out "You want to fuck somebody up? There goes a white boy; go get him".

Distinguishing *Mitchell* from *RAV*, the Court noted the Wisconsin statute punished conduct, not content that posed special harm to the individual, secondary victims and the community at large. *Mitchell* legitimated the discriminatory selection model and thereafter penalty enhancement statutes have been enacted throughout the United States. However, opponents of hate crime statutes and First Amendment scholars criticize the *Mitchell* decision positing constitutional issues, practical barriers and unintended consequences that undermine the purpose of hate crime statutes.

First Amendment Challenges: Hate Crime Statutes are Overbroad

First Amendment challenges to hate crime statutes based on claims that the statutes are overbroad have not been successful. The claim of an overbroad chilling effect of the St. Paul, Minnesota ordinance was presented in RAV; however, to the chagrin of legal scholars and philosophers, the Court did not even rule on the overbreadth claim. The overbreadth claim was precluded by the decision that ordinance was not content neutral. Still, several scholars, and concurring opinions, in RAV thought the petitioner's overbreadth claim had merit. Essentially, the Court in RAV asserted that the ordinance impermissibly proscribed protected and unprotected activities; thus the ordinance produced a chilling effect on the exercise of protected speech and activities. Consequently, citizens would be afraid to utter other constitutionally protected unpopular words or join constitutionally protected unpopular groups for fear of a later hate crime prosecution.

Initially, the Minnesota Supreme Court rejected the overbreadth claim by narrowly interpreting the St. Paul ordinance to apply only to "fighting words" that were unprotected within the meaning of Chaplinsky v. New Hampshire (315 U.S. 568) (1942). In a departure from settled First Amendment doctrine, the Court accepted the Minnesota Supreme Court's narrow definition of fighting words thus precluding the necessity of deciding overbreadth claim. However, by accepting the fighting word doctrine for use in a cross burning case, the Court tacitly expanded the context and applicability of the fighting word doctrine. Consequently, some legal scholars have criticized the Court's acceptance of the Minnesota Supreme Court's definition of "fighting words" as an expansion beyond the meaning contemplated in Chaplinsky. In RAV, the Court's acceptance of the Minnesota interpretation expanded the "fighting words" doctrine beyond the limits of face-to-face confrontation prescribed in Chaplinsky.

Another criticism of the expansion of the "fighting words" doctrine in *RAV* is that it is inconsistent with the Courts later clarification of the fighting words as words "directed to the person of the hearer" (Cohen v. California 403 U.S. 15, 1971) in a way inherently likely to provoke violent reactions. The cross burning in *RAV* did not include the face-to-face situation contemplated in Chaplinsky. Thus, critics of the decision contend the expansion of the fighting words doctrine is an unnecessary intrusion on settled First Amendment doctrine. Other critics of the RAV decision and the concurring opinions of Justices White and Blackmun have also expressed grave doctrinal concern that the Court should have decided the case within traditional First Amendment jurisprudence that laws should not chill protected speech and associations.

In the concurring opinions, the Justices White and Blackmun posited the ordinance impermissibly overbroad, likely to have a chilling effect on protected speech and activities and would invariably confuse the lower courts. Finally, opponents of hate crime statutes who argue the overbreadth claim, lament basing a hate crime conviction almost exclusively on constitutionally protected activities that comes perilously close to punishing those activities themselves (Gerstenfeld 2013).

The overbreadth argument was again before the Court in Mitchell wherein the appellant challenged that the Wisconsin statute had a chilling effect on free speech. Essentially, Mitchell claimed the Wisconsin statute was overbroad because evidence of the defendant's prior speech or associations could be used to prove that the defendant intentionally selected his victim on account of the victim's protected status. Consequently, Mitchell asserted the statute impermissibly chilled free expression for those concerned about the future possibility of enhanced sentences if they should commit a criminal offense covered by the statute. However, the Court ruled against the appellant asserting the sort of chill envisioned by a citizen suppressing his bigoted beliefs now, for fear that those beliefs will become evidence at later trial, is far more unlikely than that contemplated in traditional overbreadth cases.

Fourteenth Amendment Equal Protection and Due Process Concerns

Critics of hate crime statutes contend that these statutes also violate the Fourteenth Amendment right to equal protection and due process (Jacobs and Potter 1998; Tatchell 2002; Gellman 1992/1993). They argue that injuries to bias victims are not more severe than non-bias crime victims, and thus special protection of select victims reflects nothing more than identity politics (Jacobs and Potter 1998). Other legal scholars raise equal protection and due process concerns charging the hate crime statutes neglects to protect some citizens and are unconstitutionally vague (Morsch 1992; Gellman 1992/1993; ADL 2012). Equal Protection challenges are based on the contention that hate crime statutes unconstitutionally benefit minorities because minorities are more likely to be victims of bias crimes. Moreover, they argue that the Equal Protection Clause proscribes different treatment by government of similarly situated persons based upon their exercise of fundamental rights including those articulated in the First Amendment. As a result, persons who have committed the same offense, including a conduct offense, cannot be punished differently based solely on their thoughts or beliefs regarding the offense (Gellman 1992/1993). Critics presenting the Equal Protection argument also contend that hate crime statutes unconstitutionally burden majority members since majority members are more likely to be arrested (ADL 2012). The Equal Protection argument has not been successful because hate crime statutes require the commission of an underlying crime. The Court in *Mitchell* did not address the 14th Amendment Equal Protection argument.

The 14th amendment Due Process challenges to hate crime statutes argue poor statutory construction and ambiguity of the language drafted in discriminatory selection statutes. Moreover, opponents argue discriminatory selection statutes are impermissibly vague with respect to the behavior they proscribe and the amount of motive necessary to sustain a hate crime charge (Morsch 1992; Gellman 1992/1993). The due process clause requires that criminal statutes give clear notice of what activity is proscribed and provide adequate guidelines to prevent arbitrary law enforcement actions (ADL 2012). The clause is meant to ensure that laws are fair in substance and in implementation. Essentially, Due Process challenges claim the law is so vague as to lead an ordinary person to be uncertain of their meaning (Gerstenfeld 2013). Often the claim is about the terminology within the statute such as "color," "intentionally selects" "harasses" (ADL 2012; Gerstenfeld 2013). Alternatively, claims may be made about the statute as a whole such as the level of culpability required in mixed motive cases or the evidentiary requirement for penalty enhancement statutes (Gellman 1992/1993).

Motive and the Mental State of the Hate Crime Offender

Hate crime statutes, regardless of whether drafted on the basis of discriminatory selection or racial animus models of culpability challenge core First Amendment doctrines. Constitutional scholars debate the legitimacy of hate crime statutes with the contention that they equate motive with conduct and consequently impermissibly regulate thought in violation of the First Amendment (Jacobs and Potter 1998; Gellman 1992/1993; Goldberger 1992/1993; Jacoby 2002; Philips 2002). They allege that hate crime statutes impermissibly criminalize viewpoints, and inappropriately, often inaccurately, suggests racist motive (Morsch 1992) and unconstitutionally regulate thought (Jacobs and Potter 1998). Opponents contend hate crimes statutes present a fundamental violation of an important precept of the first amendment; that is, hate crime statutes criminalize unpopular viewpoints. They contend generic criminal laws already punish injurious conduct; consequently recriminalization or sentencing enhancement for the same injurious conduct when motivated by hate amounts to extra punishment for values, beliefs and opinions the government deems abhorrent (Jacobs and Potter 1998).

In R.A.V. v. City of St. Paul, Minnesota, the Court addressed this matter by ruling that the City of St. Paul, Minnesota bias crime ordinance was unconstitutional for including statutory language that violated the principle of content neutrality. In essence, the St. Paul ordinance was drafted to protect certain favored bias categories but not others the municipality did not favor. The Court acknowledged the government could criminalize constitutionally unprotected fighting words, but insisted that government could not exclusively criminalized fighting words that express ideas that the government thought inappropriate.

The inference of a racist motive also presents another first amendment issue. Hate crimes, like other crimes, require proof of a guilty mind reflected by "mens rea" elements of purpose, knowledge, or recklessness. However, penalty enhancement statutes require proof that the accused attacked his victim "because of" or "by reason of" a protected victim category such as race, religion, nationality etc. Morsch (1992) posits that the problem in proving racist motives is derived from the amorphous nature of motive itself. Motive is the cause of ones actions, whether one adopts a means to achieve desired ends or consciously selects those ends (p. 666). However, motive is largely determined by offenders' personality and psyche that, by and large, is inherently subjective. Thus, policing hate crimes is often contingent upon circumstantial evidence to assist first responding police officers and prosecutors in the inference of racist motives. However, proving racist motive from the circumstantial evidence, from all other possible motives, is a feat nearly impossible for prosecutors (Morsch 1992).

Lawrence (2009) argues hate crimes should be punished more but not necessarily because of the discriminatory selection or the end results of the bias action. He contends the difficulty in prosecuting hate crimes stems from the language of penalty enhancement statutes that look to the end result "because of" or "by reason of" protected bias categories. Lawrence (2009) posits that the most compelling basis for deciding if an individual has committed a bias crime is the mental state of the actor. The state of mind, or the culpability of the accused reflects the degree of guilt. Further, a focus on the results of a perpetrators action would make all offenders equally liable regardless whether they were less culpable evident by their absence of racial motivation.

The most significant constitutional issue raised by the statutory construction of discriminatory selection statutes is the evidentiary requirement of motive. Whether retributivist or utilitarian, punishment theorists, agree that the mental state of the offenders is fundamental to the issue of culpability. However, discriminatory selection hate crime statutes, per Wisconsin, merely require selection of a victim from a protected class of citizens as evidence of proscribed conduct for a hate crime prosecution.

The Problem of over Inclusiveness: Non-purposeful, Unknowing and Unconscious Hate Crimes

Many legal scholars and philosophers contend that "effect driven" or the "result oriented focus" of hate crime legislation like discriminatory selection statutes are over inclusive essentially because they equate discriminatory conduct to motive without the mental state of animus to establish culpability (Gellman 1992/1993; Maldonado 1992/1993; Lawrence 2009). Lawrence (2009) posits discriminatory selection statutes refocus the guilt from the accused mental state or culpability to the results of his conduct. Consequently, guilt may be triggered by circumstances beyond the control of the accused. According to Lawrence (2009):

> A results-oriented focus is particularly inappropriate for determining guilt in the context of bias crimes. In many cases, the harms associated with bias crimes depend entirely on whether the victim, the target group, and society perceives the perpetrator's motivations (p. 65).

Clearly, the harm based guilt standard reflected in discriminatory selections statutes allow punishment for harm caused from bias crimes even when the offending act was devoid of racial motivation as long as the target community perceived it to be racially motivated. Gellman (1992/1993) challenged the *Mitchell* court's decision arguing that the Wisconsin statute proscribed conduct protected by the First amendment. She argued that as motive consists solely of the defendant's thoughts, the additional penalty for motive amounts to a thought crime offensive to the First Amendment. Moreover, she challenged proponents of hate crime statutes perspective that motive is no different than intent or purpose, Gellman (1992/1993) countered a fundamental difference exist between intent, motive and purpose. Motive is the reason why the offender forms the intent to commit the act; intent and purpose affect what the defendant is doing; motive is why he or she is doing it. Arguably, one could have a bias motive but no intent. Moreover, in punishing a "purpose," or defendant's "beliefs" on an issue, the government is still punishing the defendant's viewpoint and opinion. The element of motive, comparable to purpose, expresses ideological content and disapproved views, and undoubtedly has a definite relationship with communication. Critics of the *Mitchell* decision argue that by not acknowledging the distinction between motive and actual conduct, the Court approved treating speech and conduct as indistinguishable elements of criminal conduct although they are quite distinguishable (Goldberger 1992/1993). Moreover, the *Mitchell* Court's failure lies within the refusal to acknowledge that the mental processes which form motives for crimes are indistinguishable from political beliefs and opinions (Goldberger 1992/1993). Gellman (1992/1993) posited that when governments punish thoughts or opinions, whether in the context of motive, purpose or conduct, it offends the same First Amendment values. Further, a governmental purpose to punish or regulate any type of content viewpoint or opinion is just as inappropriate in a pure conduct case as it is in a speech case.

Unintended Consequences of Hate Crime Legislation: Citizen Resentment, Social Backlash, Proliferation of Prejudice and Disproportionate Prosecution of Minorities

Opponents of hate crime statutes also argue that these statutes may conceivably generate unintended consequences contrary to the purposes of the legislation (Minow 1991; Grattet and Jenness 2001; Gerstenfeld 2013). These critics argue hate crime statutes are impractical and an unnecessary consequence of identity politics that emerged in the 1980s and 1990s. Jacobs and Potter (1998) described identity politics as "a politics whereby individuals relate to one another as members of competing groups based on characteristics such as race, gender, sex orientation or religion" (p. 5). Further, they contended hate crime statutes are symbolic request for special treatment by advocacy groups for materiel and symbolic reasons that are provided for by politicians for political reasons. Interestingly, Jacobs and Potter (1998) rationalize that there is value in being recognized as disadvantaged and victimized because the greater the group's victimization, the greater the moral claim on society.

Gerstenfeld (2013) lamented the broad net cast by the discriminatory selection models and raised the possibility that the addition of more groups to protected status may fuel paradoxical effects including citizen backlash and accusations of identity politics. Dixon and Gadd (2014) posited the use of prejudice statutes on behalf of exclusive minority groups conceivably could create a prejudice hierarchy, whereby some prejudice experiences are valued more than others. They posited the emergence of a prejudice hierarchy is a consequence of selecting certain characteristics for protection while ignoring others. Several scholars and practitioners have argued the "exclusive" nature of special group protection embodied with hate crime statutes has garnered resentment of minorities from groups excluded from protection (Gellman 1992/1993; Gerstenfeld 1992). Gellman (1992/1993) explained the effect of the resentment against minorities included under the protective cover of the statute is comparable to children disliking the teacher's pet for receiving special privileges. Gerstenfeld (2013) added that extremist organizations often exploit this angle in recruitment by asserting that laws are only protecting minorities. Crocker (1992/1993) posited that outside of moral reasons for privileging one group, in lieu of another, this type of legislation creates a perception of arbitrariness to the criminal law (p. 501). Further, hate crimes statutes conceivably undermine the purposes behind the law by giving prominence to the divisions the statute enumerates. Interestingly, Franklin's (1996, 1998) interview with hate crime offenders who were prosecuted under penalty enhancement statutes detected support for Crocker's concern. She found that prosecution of hate offenders under penalty enhancement statutes actually deepened resentment against minorities and increased offender's beliefs that they were oppressed by a more powerful social group and Worse, she noted the likelihood of penalty enhancement statutes increasing prejudice against minorities is greater when the offender is subject to a prison sentence where racism and homophobia is normative. Other opponents argue hate crime laws extend identity politics to crime and punishment and hence, redefine the crime problem as another venue for conflict between races, genders and nationality groups. Consequently, in lieu of unifying heterogeneous groups, hate crimes statutes polarize and create unnecessary inequalities that often breed unintended consequences. Grattet and Jenness (2001) asserted that hate crime statutes potentially "reinforces perception of target groups as ultimately less credible participants in an array of social activities, especially those interfacing with the criminal justice system" (p. 655).

Determining which group's vulnerability warrant special hate crime status protection is difficult because of the social and policy implications of excluding groups. Conceivably, for every plausible reason for enacting hate crime statutes, there are neutralizing social consequences. Minow (1991) referenced this as the "dilemma of difference" noting "problems of inequality can be exacerbated both by treating members of minority groups the same as members of the majority and by treating the two groups differently" (p. 20). On the one hand, selecting groups for protection while excluding others exposes them to the societal consequences unintended by the legislation; on the other hand, not protecting victims highly susceptible to hate motivated violence appears nonresponsive to increasing evidence of bias motivated violence disproportionately prevalent and severely injurious to vulnerable victim groups. Hate crime statutes also present practical dilemmas to law enforcement that diminish their ability to enforce society's goal of equality and social cohesion. Jenness (2002) argued that hate crime statutes are constructed with a "norm of sameness" positing the generalized construction of hate crime statutes minimizes the history of vulnerable group victimization experiences. Consequently, the victimization history and original basis for hate crime statute is obscured. Jenness (2002) noted:

> Hate Crime laws are written in a way that elides the historical basis and meaning of such crimes by translating specific categories of persons (Blacks, Jews, Gays, Lesbians, Mexicans) into all encompassing neutral categories (race, religion, sex orientation, and national origin). In doing so, the laws do not offer these groups any remedies and protections that are not simultaneously available to all other races, religions, genders, sexual orientations, nationalities, and so on (pp. 24–25).

Another consequence of the broad victimization category reflected in the statutory construction of hate crime statutes has been the increase in the prosecution of minorities, the victims these statutes were drafted to protect (Franklin 2002; Dixon and Gadd 2014) Evidence of the disproportionate prosecution of minorities is available through review of 2012 FBI UCR and NCVS reports. For instance, in 2012, African-Americans comprised 12 % of the U.S. population yet 23.3 % of known hate crime offenders according to the United States Department of Justice 2012 Hate Crime Statistics report. Similarly, Strom (2001) analysis of NIBRS aggravated assaults between 1997 and 1999 reflected African-American male and female offenders comprised 20 and 6 %, respectively, of all the hate offender characteristics by the most serious offense type. Moreover, Wilson's (2014) victimization analysis also indicated that African Americans comprised 32 % of the perception by victims of the race of the offenders.[1] Evidence of this trend was also detected by a 1993 Southern Poverty Leadership Conference (SPLC) study indicated 46 % of killings motivated by race were committed by African Americans offenders (Appleborne 1993). SPLC concluded that hate crime violence by African American were escalating at an alarming rate. Gerstenfeld (2013) described the burgeoning arrest and prosecution of minorities as hate offenders as "disempowering" Perhaps this is one of the ramifications of the decision in RAV. v. City of St. Paul. More specifically, contemporary hate crime legislation has been drafted with broad based bias categories in lieu of specific bias types to overcome potential content neutrality and equal protection challenges. However, it is important to note that contemporary hate crime legislation enacted to equally proscribe and protect against anti-White and anti-Black bias appears to have disparate and adverse impact on Black offenders.

Finally, complacency by politicians who previously adopted less stringent hate crime policies has produced a potential adverse effect against drafting more stringent hate crime legislation (Soule and Earl 2001; Gerstenfeld 2013). Essentially, early enactment of less effective hate crime legislation has often produced a buffer effect whereby states that initially enacted data collection or civil rights statutes tended to be slower to adopt more stringent hate crime enforcement laws (Soule and Earl 2001). Consequently, politicians are not nearly as expedient to address prejudice in other social arenas such as housing, education, and employment. Soule and Earl (2001) concluded early enactment of data collection and civil rights statutes deflected pressure to pass later measures of equality; consequently, enactments of important protections for victims have been slow.

Hate crime statutes generate a plethora of opposing viewpoint regarding their relative advantages and disadvantages. Policy makers are presented with a clear set of policy dilemmas undoubtedly not contemplated when the statutes were drafted. Perhaps Minow (1991) conceptualized it best. We are faced with a "dilemma of difference".

---

[1]The NCVS special report by Wilson (2014) does not indicate whether the offenders were prosecuted.

References

ADL. (2012). Hate Crime Laws.

Appleborne, P. (1993, December 13). Rise is found in hate crimes committed by blacks. The New York Times, p. A12.

Chaplinski v. New Hampshire (1942). U.S. Supreme Court, 315 U.S. 568.

Cohen v. California. (1971). U.S. Supreme Court, 403 U.S. 15.

Crocker, L. (1992/1993). Hate crime statutes: Just? constitutional? wise?. *Annual Survey of American Law 485.*

Dixon, B., & Gadd, D. (2014). Look before you leap: Hate crime legislation reconsidered. *South African Crime Quarterly, 40*, 25–30.

Franklin, K. (1996). *Hate crime or rite of passage?: Assailant motivations in antigay violence* (Doctoral dissertation).

Franklin, K. (1998) Unassuming motivations; contextualizing the narratives of antigay assailants. In G. M. Herek (Ed.), (1997), *Stigma and sexual orientation: Understanding prejudice against lesbians, gay men and bisexuals* (Vol. 4). Sage Publications.

Franklin, K. (2002). Good intentions: The enforcement of hate crime penalty-enhancement statutes. *American Behavioral Scientist, 46*, 154–172.

Gellman, S. (1992/1993). Hate crime laws are thought crime laws. *Annual Survey of American Law*, 509.

Gerstenfeld, P. B. (1992). Smile when you call me that! The problems with punishing hate motivated behavior. *Behavioral Sciences and the Law, 10*, 259–285.

Gerstenfeld, P. B. (2013). *Hate crimes: Causes, controls, and controversies*. Sage.

Goldberger, D. (1992/1993). Hate crime laws and their impact on the first amendment. *Annual Survey of American Law*, 569.

Grattet, R., & Jenness, V. (2001). Examining the boundaries of hate crime law: Disabilities and the dilemma of difference. *Journal of Criminal Law and Criminology, 91*, 653.

Jacobs, J. B., & Potter, K. (1998). *Hate crimes: Criminal law & identity politics* (Vol. 67). New York: Oxford University Press.

Jacoby J. (2002). Punish crime not thought crime In P. Iganski (Ed.), *The hate debate: Should hate be punished as a crime* (pp. 114–122). London: The Institute for Jewish Policy Research.

Jenness, V. (2002). Contours of hate crime politics and law in the United States. In P. Iganski (Ed.), *The Hate Debate: should hate be punished as a crime* (pp. 15–35). London: The Institute for Jewish Policy Research.

Lawrence, F. M. (2009). *Punishing hate: Bias crimes under American law*. Harvard University Press.

Maldonado, M. (1992/1993). Practical problems with enforcing hate crime legislation in New York. *Annual Survey of American Law, 555.*

Minow, M. (1991). *Making all the difference: Inclusion, exclusion, and American law*. Cornell University Press.

Morsch, J. (1992). The problem of motive in hate crimes: The argument against presumptions of racial motivation. *The Journal of Criminal Law and Criminology, 82*(3), 659–689.

Philips, M. (2002). Hate crime: the Orwellian response to prejudice. In P. Iganski (Ed.), *The hate debate: Should hate be punished as a crime* (pp. 123–131). London: The Institute for Jewish Policy Research.

R.A.V. v. City of St. Paul Minnesota. (1992). U.S. Supreme Court, 505 U.S. 377.

Soule, S. A., & Earl, J. (2001). The enactment of state-level hate crime law in the United States: Intrastate and interstate factors. *Sociological Perspectives, 44*(3), 281–305.

Strom, K. (2001). *Hate crimes reported in NIBRS, 1997–99*. US Department of Justice, Office of Justice Programs, Bureau of Justice Statistics.

Tatchell, P. (2002). *Some people are more equal than others in the hate debate: Should hate be punished as a crime* (pp. 54–70). London: The Institute for Jewish Policy Research.

United States Department of Justice, Federal Bureau of Investigation. (2014, December). *Hate Crime Statistics, 2012*. Retrieved 3 September 2015 from https://www.fbi.gov/about-us/cjis/ucr/hate-crime/2012/tables-and-data-declarations/1tabledatadecpdf/table_1_incidents_offenses_victims_and_known_offenders_by_bias_motivation_2012.xls.

Wilson, M. (2014). *Hate crime victimizations, 2004–2012-statistical tables*. Bureau of Justice Statistics, National Crime Victimization Survey.

Wisconsin v. Mitchell. (1993). U.S. Supreme Court, 505 U.S. 476.

Chapter 7
The Law Enforcement and Prosecution Dilemma

Factors that Influence Police Departments Interpretations and Reporting of Hate Crimes

The enforcement of hate crime statutes generally begins with the first level law enforcement officer arriving as the first responder to the potential bias crime incident. After determining the presence of probable cause of a criminal act, the officer is faced with the decision of whether to classify the case as a hate crime. However, numerous factors influence the officer's bias classification decision. According to Nolan and Akijama (1999), police agency and personal and individual factors influence the likelihood of reporting and recording hate crime incidents. Nolan and Akijama (1999) specify the hate crime data collection process at the police agency level delineating four steps: First, victims report hate crimes incident; second, police officer's record incident as a hate crime; and third, police determine and verify hate incident and fourth police agencies participate in the hate crime reporting program. They note the second step involving the influence of personal and individual factors and the fourth step relating to police–agency factors as potential sources that may explain police underreporting.

Personal and individual police officers factors include attitudes and beliefs about the necessity of hate-defined offenses; the perception of the necessity for the additional workload; and the uselessness of reporting. Personal factors and beliefs also influence reporting at the police agency level. These include the officer's personal beliefs, training and the rank and file attitudes of other police officers (Martin 1996; Cronin et al. 2007). In agencies without a specified hate crime enforcement policy, the first responding police officer's personal belief in the necessity of hate crime laws weighs heavily in his classification decision (Levin 1999; Nolan and Akijama 1999). Nolan and Akijama's (1999) found that the first responding police officer's personal beliefs includes whether the officer believes hate crime reporting is actually effective; whether the officer thought it was the job of the police to report hate crimes; and the officer's perception of whether hate

© The Author(s) 2017

F.S. Pezzella, *Hate Crime Statutes*, SpringerBriefs in Policing,
DOI 10.1007/978-3-319-40842-2_7

crimes was really a problem. In addition, workload issues such as busy caseloads and reticence by victims to cooperate in the investigation and prosecution also influenced the first responding police officer's classification decision. Victim reluctance to cooperate or even report bias crime incidents was found to discourage the first responding officer from accurately classifying bias incidents. Thus, the first responding police officer's personal beliefs are highly influential in the classification decision and ultimately to reporting the prevalence and nature of hate crime victimizations.

A number of other internal and external police agency factors have also been found to bear on the first responding police officer's classification. These include budget retrenchment and reduction in services during periods of increased demand. These factors often preclude the perceived luxury of a resource-intensive bias crime detection unit. Consequently, external factors such as undesirable fiscal circumstances conceivably may influence both police administration and rank and file police officers' perception of the praticality of bias crime investigations. bias crime investigations as impractical, where retrenchment of police officers result in a loss of personnel the chances of misclassification bias incidents is even greater.

Finally, cohesion with the local community is an additional factor which bears on the officer normative evaluation of whether classifying and reporting the incident as a hate crime will make things better or worse for the community; or the victim (Nolan and Akijama 1999). Police agency factors include whether the local police department perceives hate crime reporting as consistent with community beliefs and usefulness of hate crime reporting in strengthening ties to the community; also, whether police involvement in identifying hate crimes will have a positive effect.

The Effect of Police Departments Variations in Training

Nolan and Akijama (1999) found that the absence of supportive organizational policies and practices and commitment primarily mostly demonstrated by supportive law enforcement training influenced the likelihood of classifying and reporting hate crime. Invariably, if the local police agency does not perceive hate crimes as a priority, only limited and scarce police resources will be allocated to hate crime training. The presence of hate crime training has been found to influence the classification decision and likelihood of reporting. Several hate crime scholars have noted that definitive organizational hate crime enforcement policies sensitize police to enforcing and reporting hate crimes (Martin 1996; Nolan and Akijama 1999). To that extent, police agencies that provide or allow access to hate crime investigation training reflect the organizational commitment to enforcement of hate crime statutes that increases the likelihood of hate crime reporting. However, actual and access to hate crime training has been found to vary significantly among police agencies. Walker and Katz (1995) surveyed 16 separate police department bias units and found substantial variation in the departments commitment to enforcing bias crime laws. Only half of the departments provided law enforcement officers with any kind of specialized hate crime investigation training. Further, four departments who reported bias crime units actually did not have one. Nolan et al. (2004) suggest police need to develop professional vision to "see" bias crimes particularly in the most prevalent types of mixed or secondary motive bias crime cases that are often perceived by the officer as ambiguous. Further, they posit that ambiguity in bias crime reporting is a major source of confusion and frustration within law enforcement invariably contributing to erroneous national hate crime statistics. They conclude that training is critical to accurate classification and reporting of hate crimes.

Investigation Issues: The Classification Decision of Bias Motivation

The FBI lists 14 separate bias crime indicators (See Appendix) to assist law enforcement in the classification of the bias crime incident (Hate Crime Data Collection Guidelines and Training Manual, version 2.0 2015). Still, the first decision of the responding first level law enforcement officer upon assessing probable cause of criminal conduct concerns the classification of a suspected bias motivated crime. Do the victims meet the jurisdiction's hate crime statutory criteria for protected groups? The detection of bias indicators will help secure the requisite probable cause of bias motivation. However, the responding officer must be knowledgeable of the states' prescribed protected victim categories.

Although not necessarily germane to the officer at time of arrest, an understanding of the states' evidentiary requirements to establish probable cause of a bias crime motivation is also important.[1] State statutes vary substantively in the weight of evidence required to establish the presence of the proscribed bias motivation. Delaware, Maryland, Vermont, Virginia, and Wisconsin incorporate discriminatory selection as the requisite evidentiary criteria of bias. Minimally, these states require victim selection of a protected bias victim category to support probable cause for a bias crime arrest. However, other states such as Connecticut, Florida, Massachusetts, New Hampshire, and New Jersey require proof of racial animus. Although both types of bias crime statutes may include the "because of" "by reason of," motivational phrasing to identify protected groups, the animus statute states also require evidence of maliciousness, prejudice, or hostility. Grattet and Jenness (2001) posited that four distinct motivational phrasings are present throughout the body of U.S. hate crime statutes. Moreover, they note the language of the statute reflect the motivational phrasing popular at the time of the initial enactment. Statutes incorporating the "because of," "intent to intimidate or harass,"

[1]Pursuant to FBI UCR guidelines, it is recommended that police agencies adopt a two tiered bias investigation process with first and second level judgment officers.

"maliciously and with specific intent to harass," and "prejudice, hostility, and maliciousness" motivational phrasing reflect varying levels of racial animus, and thus increasing difficulty for the law enforcement officer responsible for making the classification decision.

The typical bias crime incident is quite difficult to discern. Recall, McDevitt's et al. (2002) typology of bias offenders inclusive of four conceptually different bias motivations with varying levels of culpability. Also, consider the culpability of the mixed/peripheral bias motivated offender (Frielich and Chermak 2013). Under McDevitt et al. (2002) typology of offenders, mission, thrill-seeking, defensive and retaliatory hate offenses reflect very different levels of culpability concerning bias motivation. This is vitally important because the majority of bias incidents that rise to the level of a criminal complaint, the true bias motivation is often unclear. Of the 600 cases McDevitt et al. (2002) assessed under his typology thrill seeking constituted (66 %) and defensive hate crime comprised (25 %) of all types of hate crimes. McDevitt et al. (2002) noted only one percent of his cases reflected the characteristics of true hate "mission" offender as defined in the typology. Therefore, the majority (91 %) of typical bias incidents are those that arrive before the first responding police officer with unclear, mixed, and secondary motivations as delineated by Freilich and Chermak (2013). Under these circumstances, the causal connection between the offender's bias motivation and culpability is not always evident for the first responding police officer to discern. The first responding officer must look for evidence of bias indicators BUT also offender culpability that reflects bias toward a legally protected categories of victims (Mason 2014). Therefore, the immediate dilemma presented to the officer is to determine whether an otherwise ordinary criminal incident contains evidence indicative of bias conduct to properly classify or refer the case as a bias crime.

Typically, bias indicators may be present upon a cursory observation of the scene; however, further investigation may reveal the absence of malice, hostility, or prejudice toward any statutorily protected group. In states that incorporate the discriminatory selection threshold for bias crime statutes, a bias motivated arrest and prosecution is permissible by the mere presence of selection bias even in the absence of group antipathy by the offender. For the first responding police officer, this is administratively convenient to support a bias motivated arrest (Adams 2005). However, in cases of mixed and secondary motivations, the officer is faced with a critical classification decision regarding the type of arrest. There are three possibilities for consideration. First, make the arrest and the bias classification decision in the face of an obvious flaw in the statute that criminalizes selection without group antipathy. Second, arrest in spite of case being perceived as weak because of secondary and partial motivations and the lack of clarity relative to the weight of mixed bias and non-biased motivations within the same criminal incident. Or third, ignore the indicators and make the arrest for a non-bias motivated crime consistent with the officer's gut and subjective state of mind regarding the motive of the offender. Again, the classification decision of first responding police officer is difficult because the circumstances surrounding the bias incident are unclear and difficult to discern.

Deciphering Mixed and Secondary Bias Motivations

The bias investigation officer or prosecutor must decipher evidence of the bias motivation including whether racial, ethnic, anti-religious, or anti-gay/lesbian slurs or utterances preceded the biased conduct; or whether such biased utterances followed a previous non-biased incident that escalated into heated words and ultimately the appearance of biased conduct (Maldonado 1992/1993). This is important because bias is often a secondary motive (Martin 1996; Maldonado 1992/1993).

Consider the facts in State of Ohio v. Wyant 64 Ohio St. 3d 566 (1992). Two campers occupying campsites adjacent to one another had a dispute about the volume of music late at night. The dispute escalated into a physical altercation and the White camper used racial epithets while assaulting the African American camper. The defense for the White camper claimed there was no race bias motivation or animus towards Black people; the defendant offered proof in the form of names of friends who were black to refute the bias complaint. The prosecution challenged the quality of the defendant's interracial relationships to refute the defendant's claim of non-bias motivation. Lawrence (1999) asserted the issue should turn on the culpability or the state of mind of the offender. This issue is the fundamental dilemma presented to the first responding officer.

To explicate this point, variation in the culpability of three hypothetical bias offenders was presented by Lawrence (1999) to illuminate the potential for over inclusiveness in discriminatory selection statutes. First, he described the clever bias criminal who is fully aware of the centrality of his culpability and guilt for the bias crime incident. Therefore, the clever bias criminal asserts a pretextual non-bias motivation reason for perhaps, an assault that was in fact, motivated by bias. The clever bias criminal easily coincides with the description of the mission offender under the (McDevitt et al. 2002) expanded typology. The clever bias criminal's mission and purpose is to promote and maintain racial and/or religious superiority and inferiority through publically notorious acts of bias motivated violence toward primary direct and secondary indirect victims. However, what makes the clever bias criminal clever is the fact that he does not wish to publically acknowledge his mission although he is satisfied with the notoriety and delivery of his hate message. He is likely aware of the severity of sanctions associated with his bias conduct but he does not incriminate himself by revealing his bias motivation. His conduct exhibits feigned ignorance of the particularly injurious nature of the hurt he causes his victim. The first level responding officer at the scene of a potential bias incident discovers bias indicators. The clever bias criminal articulates a non-bias motive to avoid being charged with a bias crime (Lawrence 1999). His disguise obscures his bias motivation and typically the investigating officer arriving at the crime scene may not readily observe the true state of mind; the bias motivated animus of the clever bias criminal. However, further investigation and the acquisition of evidence will reveal the clever bias criminal's true state of mind.

The second hypothetical illustrating culpability is that of the unconscious racist. The unconscious racist perpetrates a bias motivated crime perhaps an interracial assault. The unconscious racist is unconsciously motivated by bias and thus without racial motivation or animus. He or she asserts the victim improperly strayed in his neighborhood and that, regardless of the victim's ethnicity, he would have attacked him to defend his turf. The unconscious racist actually believes this assertion. The unconscious racist presents a far more complicated problem with respect to the issue of mental state of the offender. Lawrence (1999) noted that unlike the clever bias criminal, the reasons reported by the unconscious racist for his conduct are not consciously pre-textual. The unconscious racist claims he is a conscious defender of his turf from outsiders; his unconscious motivation is to keep some statutorily protected group out of his neighborhood but is unaware of his or her unconscious motivation.

Should the unconscious racist be found guilty of an unconscious bias crime? According to Lawrence (1999), the unconscious racist is not guilty of a bias crime because punishment based on a person's unconscious motives runs afoul of the principle of voluntariness that underpins the criminal law. More specifically, a person may only be punished for what he did of his own volition. In the case of the unconscious racist, he did not voluntarily attack his victim for racial reasons nor is his conscious reasons for doing so to inflict the particular harm associated with bias crime. Moreover, Lawrence (1999) asserts that evidentiary problems concerning the precise nature of the defendant's unconsciousness are difficult to overcome and warrant the defendant be found not guilty of a bias crime.

Finally, Lawrence (1999) described the behavior and culpability of the unknowing offensive actor. The unknowing offensive actor seeks to shock or offend the community generally but does so in a way that is threatening to a particular statutorily protected group. Typically, he or she may deface public property with a burning cross or Nazi swastika because he or she knows that the use of the societal taboos will shock people in general. However, he or she neither intends to offend African Americans or Jews nor is he aware of the significance of the burning cross or swastika to either of these protected groups. The unknowing offensive actor reflects the least amount of animus towards the victim. Unknowing offensive actors are often young offenders who commit hate crimes, primarily vandalism, for the thrill or shock value. These are perpetrators who do not specifically seek to offend the victim particularly or their community and are generally unaware that their conduct has this effect. The offender consciously acts intentionally to cause harm associated with the parallel crime of vandalism but in the process cause harm associated with a bias crime.

All three bias offenders share the fact that they caused harm associated with a bias crime. However, unlike the clever bias criminal, the unknowing offensive actor does not intentionally cause the harm of a bias crime; nor does he or she seek to unconsciously cause the harm of a bias crime like the unconscious racist. Because of the absence of animus within the state of mind of the unknowing offensive actor, he or she is not a bias criminal. However, the unknowing bias criminal would be found guilty of vandalism.

According to Lawrence (1999), the least problematic of the three is the clever bias offender. The proof of bias motivation is not unlike the proof of other types of motivation. Although difficult, the prosecution may incorporate circumstantial evidence that may give rise to the inference of racial motivation. More specifically, circumstantial evidence in conjunction with the nature of the assault and statement by the accused may prove bias motivation. These three hypothetical cases illustrate the problems with discriminatory selection statutes. All three would be subject to prosecution under discriminatory selection criteria. However, only the clever bias criminal reflects both the motive and the conduct that statute was enacted to proscribe. Deciphering the bias culpability of the unconscious racist is considerably difficult. The unconscious racist is really unaware of his racism.

Consider the defense used in the Yusuf Hawkins, Bensonhurst, New York case. Yusef Hawkins, a African-American teenager entered into a predominantly white middle class residential neighborhood in Bensonhurst, a Brooklyn NY suburb. The defendants chased and beat Yuseff Hawkins to death while yelling racial epithets as victim fell unconscious into a comatose state. Yusef Hawkins subsequently died from the aggravated assaults and the defendants were charged with bias motivated homicide. To the bias element of the murder, the defendants claimed there was no racially biased motivation. Moreover, neighbors in the community also asserted there were no racial problems in the neighborhood and that the motive for the beating was more of turf protection from outsiders. They asserted that it is not your skin color, but whether neighborhood residents knew you that would determine whether you would be assaulted or not. First level responding police officers who encounter circumstances where unconscious racism is evident are faced with the instantaneous decision of whether turf protection, an otherwise ordinary, non-biased offense is the motivation for the offense or whether bias is the principal motivating factor.

Lawrence (1999) asserted that if a jury, or for this discussion, the police officer, is persuaded that the defendants were consciously motivated to protect their neighborhood and that the defendants were unconsciously motivated to keep African Americans out and were honestly unaware of their unconscious motivation then the arrest should not be made for a bias crime. Here, the question before the officer is whether the probable cause of a bias crime is sufficiently established by the mens rea requirement of unconscious bias motivation in addition to the criminal conduct that causes harm ordinarily associated with bias crimes.

Lawrence (1999) illustrated another hypothetical bias incident where assessing motivation or state of mind is essential to the classification and prosecution of bias crimes. The motivation of the unknowing bias offender may very well represent the most prevalent form of bias crime first and second level bias judgement investigators may encounter. Recall, McDevitt et al. (2002) thrill seeking bias crimes accounts for almost 66 % of all bias crimes. Unlike mission or defensive motivated bias offenders whose animus or hostility has a basis, thrill-seeking offenders are often followers who harbor no real animus toward potential victims. They are motivated by the excitement of the bias incident and often do not understand or appreciate the severity or uniqueness of injury they exact on victims. Consider the motivation of thrill seeking offender in light of Lawrence's (1999) description of the culpability of the unknowing bias offender. The unknowing bias offender typically commits a harm ordinarily associated with bias, with obvious bias indicators, but for an otherwise non-bias motivation. To illustrate, envision the hypothetical example of an offender who vandalizes a synagogue. The offender does not specifically seek to harm Jewish people nor does he know the unique injury the act perpetrates. The motivation for the harm is for the shock effect characteristic of thrill seeking hate crimes. The unknowing bias criminal seeks and knows only that his vandalism causes great public outcry and that is his single motivation.

As in the case of the unconscious bias offender, the first responding law enforcement officer or bias investigator must make a classification decision over the bias criminal conduct observed. Under Mitchell, in states that incorporate discriminatory selection, bias conduct reflected by selection, regardless of motivation, is eligible for a bias arrest. Yet, as often the case, it is clear to the investigating officer that the perpetrator had no or very little knowledge of the history or meaning of their conduct to the victim. For instance, thrill-seeking offenders may tag a swastika as graffiti on a synagogue but not fully understand the significance and severity of injury to Jewish people. Still, the dilemma for the police officer and the prosecutor is whether to classify the offense as a bias crime upon evidence of bias indicators although actual bias motivation is not readily apparent. The conduct that is normally associated with bias crimes is evident; however, the officer's professional assessment is that there is no bias motivation accompanying the criminal conduct. What and how does the officer decide?

Conceivably, the unknowing bias offender may be guilty of criminal negligence because he should have known that his conduct would cause a particularized harm (Lawrence 1999). However, this degree of culpability may or may not be a statutory option for the first responding police officer. The unknowing bias offender cannot be guilty of a bias crime essentially because his use of the swastika is merely by accident (Lawrence 1999). Here, the unknowing bias offender lacks key elements of culpability. That is, the offender did not purposely, knowingly and intentionally cause a bias motivated harm (Morsch 1992).

Gellman (1992/1993) depicts two other bias crime hypothetical situations to explain the difficulty of disentangling mixed motivations that trigger the hate crime event. Conceivably, her hypothetical cases describes the actions of Lawrence's (1999), unconscsious bias offender. Suppose that the offender discovers that his or her car has been vandalized and witnesses describe the suspect as a person of Asian descent. Upon learning this, the unconscious bias offender assaults the first Asian person he sees in proximity to the car. His response retaliation motivated assault involves selecting Asians merely for identification purposes. However, the triggering event was the vandalism of the car. The first responding police officer is faced with a bias indicator of "intentional selection" of protected classification of victim but clearly the bias incident is peripheral and of mixed motivation (Freilich and Chermak 2013). In addition to identifying the interracial component, the officer also understands the triggering event that set off the assault was non-bias motivated. Bias indicators are clearly present. However, the unconscious perpetrator of this response-retaliatory bias event consciously directs his anger towards people of Asian decent but without the conscious race bias motivated animus. Here, again the first level responding police officer must decide whether to classify the case as suspiciously bias motivated and call the bias investigation unit, or arrest for a non-bias motivated assault. Taken together, with all the factors that bear on the first responding police officer, it is quite clear why bias crimes are often misunderstood and misclassified.

Practical Challenges to Prosecution of Hate Crimes Offenses

As significant as the bias classification and arrest challenges are to the first responding police officer or bias investigator, prosecutors also encounter dilemmas that challenge the prosecution of hate crimes. Recall the variation in evidentiary requirements required under the three basic motivational criteria and phrasing necessary to support a bias crime classification and arrest (Grattet and Jenness 2001). Similarly, Lawrence (1999) posited U.S. bias crime statutes can be classified under a typology that included racial animus, discriminatory selection and "because of" statutes as the predominant form of U.S. bias crime legislation. Moreover, he noted that the typology of U.S. statutes represent varying levels of evidentiary burden required for proof of motivation to prosecuting hate crimes. Further, he noted animus statutes and statutes that incorporate the "because of" bias motivational phrasing require additional proof of the element of maliciousness. Thus, the prosecution of bias crimes requires the additional burden of proving bias motivation, unlike the prosecution of parallel non-bias crimes. Comparable to the dilemma encountered by the first responding police officer, the bias crime prosecutor must additionally decide whether the elevated burden of proof of bias motivation, beyond a reasonable doubt, can be attained. Some legal scholars have made a point of distinguishing the onorus burden necessary to attain a bias crime conviction. They note that the required proof of bias motive characteristic of animus statutes is not an element in the determination of guilt of parallel non-bias crimes and hence, contrary to principles of criminal liability (Morsch 1992; Mason 2014).[2]

Recall the turf protection explanation to the first responding police officer mentioned above. As often the case, the turf protection from outsiders may be a pretense. If investigators find that the potential bias offender's definition of an outsider is synonymous with Black, or other non-white races, then sufficient bias motivation can be established to support bias arrests (Lawrence 1999). However, the depth of this level of the investigation is often beyond the scope of the first responding police officer or bias investigators purview at the scene of the bias incident. Prosecutors will have to establish the link between the offenders definition

[2]The parallel non-bias crime references the same crime absent the bias motivation. For instance, aggravated assault with and without bias motivation.

of outsider bias as a synonym for race bias. This may be accomplished through the presentation of evidence indicating that when White outsiders come into the neighborhood, the offenders turf protection rationale did not apply. More specifically, evidence that white outsiders were never molested basically will undermine the offender's turf protection defense. However, should the prosecutor's investigation determine that White victims were also subject to the turf protection violence or that the defendant's unconscious bias motivation includes some or all white victims, then the prosecutor's race bias prosecution may also be compromised. Faced with the evidentiary burden, of proving beyond a reasonable doubt, a race bias motivation where there are both White offenders and victims also presents prosecutors with a significant dilemma. Prosecute the case as bias crime and risks acquittal of the offender or pursue the parallel non-bias crime counterpart where there is a high likelihood of a conviction.

From the prosecutor's viewpoint, the threshold for proving bias motivation jeopardizes the likelihood of a conviction for either the bias, or for that matter, the parallel non-bias crime. Morsch (1992) discussed the variation in mens rea requirement for bias versus non-bias motivated crimes. Traditional, non-bias mens rea statutory requirements consist of purpose, knowledge, recklessness or criminal negligence to establish the guilty mind; however, statutory requirements for animus and those statutes that incorporate the motivational phrasing "because of" or "by reason of" require circumstantial or physical evidence of the racist motive in the form of proof of animus, hostility or maliciousness or hatred of a person's identity within a statutory protected category. This proof threshold severely undermines the efficacy of animus type statutes (Lawrence 1999). Consequently, except for the most rare circumstances where bias motivation is clearly evident, prosecutors are discouraged from prosecuting hate crime charges under animus statutes. Morsch (1992) explained the primary difficulty for prosecutors and plaintiffs is that the bias motive lies primarily within the knowledge of the offender. As noted in Chap. 6, critics of hate crime statutes contend punishing hate wrongly penalizes a person's motives and the values expressed through their behavior (Gellman 1992/1993; Adams 2005). Moreover, contemporary hate crime legislation arguably criminalizes the offenders' beliefs, bad thoughts, and/or feelings, and hence breach constitutional rights to freedom of expression (Mason 2014). These types of first amendment issues, in addition to the right against self-incrimination, seriously compromise the prosecutor's ability to prove racist motives. Grattet and Jenness (2001) noted "while the animus model is desirable insofar as it targets bigotry directly, its weaker jurisprudential foundation in antidiscrimination principles render it more vulnerable to constitutional challenges" (p. 690) Consequently, typical bias cases that involve partial and secondary bias motivations are difficult to prosecute and the dilemma for prosecutor is to decide whether to prosecute as a bias complaint given the onorus proof requirement necessary for a conviction. Both Morsch (1992) and Maldonado (1992/1993) asserted the net result of such a stringent bias motivation proof requirement is the undermining of the prosecutors' ability to obtain convictions in all but the most egregious and clear cases of bias motivation.

References

Adams, D. M. (2005). Punishing hate and achieving equality. *Criminal Justice Ethics, 24*(1), 19–30.

Criminal Justice Information Services, Division of Uniform Crime Reporting Program. (2015). Hate Crime Data Collection Guidelines and Training Manual, version 2.0.

Cronin, S. W., McDevitt, J., Farrell, A., & Nolan, J. J. (2007). Bias-crime reporting organizational responses to ambiguity, uncertainty, and infrequency in eight police departments. *American Behavioral Scientist, 51*(2), 213–231.

Freilich, J. D., & Chermak, S. M. (2013). Hate Crimes. Problem-oriented guides for police, Problem-Specific Guides Series, (72).

Gellman, S. (1992/1993). Hate crime laws are thought crime laws. *Annual Survey American Law, 509*.

Grattet, R., & Jenness, V. (2001). Examining the boundaries of hate crime law: Disabilities and the dilemma of difference. *The Journal of Criminal Law and Criminology, 91*, 653.

Lawrence, F. M. (1999). *Punishing hate: Bias crimes under American law*. Harvard University Press.

Levin, B. (1999). Hate crimes worse by definition. *Journal of contemporary criminal justice, 15*(1), 6-21.

Maldonado, M. (1992/1993). Practical problems with enforcing hate crime legislation in New York. *Annual Survey American Law, 555.*

Martin, S. E. (1996). Investigating hate crimes: Case characteristics and law enforcement responses. *Justice Quarterly, 13*(3), 455–480.

Mason, G. (2014). Legislating against hate. *The Routledge International Handbook on Hate Crime, 59.*

McDevitt, J., Levin, J., & Bennett, S. (2002). Hate crime offenders: An expanded typology. *Journal of Social Issues, 58*(2), 303–317.

Morsch, J. (1992). The problem of motive in hate crimes: The argument against presumptions of racial motivation. *The Journal of Criminal Law and Criminology, 82*(3), 659–689.

Nolan, J. J., & Akijama, Y. (1999). An analysis of factors that affect law enforcement participation in hate crime reporting. *Journal of Contemporary Criminal Justice, 15*(1), 111–127.

Nolan III, J. J, McDevitt, J., Cronin, S., & Farrell, A. (2004). Learning to see hate crimes: A framework for understanding and clarifying ambiguities in bias crime classification. *Criminal Justice Studies, 17*(1), 91–105.

State of Ohio v. Wyant 64 Ohio St. 3d 566 (1992).

Walker, S., & Katz, C. M. (1995). Less than meets the eye: Police department bias crime units. *American Journal of Police, 14*, 29.

Chapter 8
Summary Discussion and Recommendations

Hate crime policy has largely been developed by the ardent advocacy of bias victim groups that lobby for severe sanctions beyond that which is provided for parallel ordinary crimes. Indeed, hate crime policy and the construction of contemporary hate crime statutes has evolved over time as political reactions to extremely violent hate motivated incidents illuminated by advocacy groups (Mason 2014). Through advocacy and activism, brutal hate motivated victimization incidents have been successfully presented before a startled public and policymakers. In the U.S., hate crime policy accelerated after notorious and extremely violent hate motivated cases were publicized. To this point, the names of the most recent federal hate crime legislation, "The Mathew Shepard and James Byrd Jr. Hate Crime Prevention Act," bears the names of two victims of extremely horrific homophobic and race bias motivated tragedies. Scholars who observed the evolution of hate crime policy in the U.S. posit the social construction of hate crimes as a policy domain came as a result of the activism of civil rights, gay and lesbian, religious freedom and crime victim movements (Grattett and Jenness 2001). Accordingly, they brought extreme cases of prejudice-motivated violence grounded in racism, sexism, homophobia, and anti-Semitism to the attention of the public and policy makers (Mason 2014). U.S. Policy makers, in turn, hasten to develop hate crime policies especially in the light of the U.S. Supreme Courts endorsement of the Wisconsin hate crime statute. Arguably, the effectiveness of group activism has spawned a piecemeal "reactive" hate crime policy that protects the interest of groups whose activism is most vocal. Moreover, as an increasing diversity of bias categories and incidents are brought to the attention of policymakers more self-defined victimized groups have been added broadening the umbrella of protection. Constructing public policy as a reaction to extreme incidents of hate crimes, at first glance, appears to be a legitimate and appropriate governmental response to safeguard citizens. However, reactionary hate crime policy formulation suffers from many unintended consequences. Commenting on this point, Mason (2014) asserted social and political advocates of hate crimes "generated a well intentioned but

© The Author(s) 2017

F.S. Pezzella, *Hate Crime Statutes*, SpringerBriefs in Policing,
DOI 10.1007/978-3-319-40842-2_8

problematic legal response to the social problem of crime that is related, in various ways, to prejudice, hostility, or intolerance of the other" (p. 59).

It is important to note that neither hate crimes nor legislation promulgated to stop hate violence is novel. The history of the U.S. reflects numerous eras of intergroup conflict characterized by hate motivated violence. To a large extent, hate motivated violence was normative when victims were other than White (Petrosino 1999). Certainly, there are lessons to be learned if we can objectively examine the continuity of hate motivated violence from the past, to the present and the future. For instance, the prevalent types of hate motivated violence throughout history centers around the bias categories of race, religion, ethnicity and sexual orientation. However, a more in depth analysis reveals that specific types of bias including anti-Black, anti-Semitism, anti-Hispanic, and anti-LGBT, violence reflect the most historically prevalent types of hate violence. Clearly, it would not be an overgeneralization to suggest that xenophobia has been institutionalized within the fabric of American society. The number of violent conflicts between Donald Trump supporters and protestors in the 2016 republican presidential campaign characterizes this type of polarization and fear of those who are different. Here, the old adage applies "if we don't learn from history we are doomed to repeat it." However, the construction of contemporary hate crime policy and corresponding statutes has not been the remedy because the history of intergroup conflict has not been comprehensively considered. To a large extent, policymakers are in denial about the severity of intergroup conflict over the life course of the country. This is quite problematic for policy makers, responding first level police officers and prosecutors. For policy makers, unintended consequences such as social backlash, potential increases in prejudice and disparate prosecution of minority groups are paradoxical effects unanticipated in the enactment of contemporary hate crime statutes. Moreover, these statutes have been enacted without provisions to encourage victims to report or to properly train police officers. Given the difficulty of assessing bias motivation, the absence of police officer training is significant with ramification on our ability to understand the scope and severity of injuries.

Future hate crime policies should incorporate a multifaceted preventive approach. First, incorporating McDevitt's and colleagues (2002) typology, the focus should be directed to youth most likely to perpetrate thrill-seeking hate crimes. Perhaps including tolerance training of those who are different and teaching about the history of intergroup conflicts throughout middle and high school curricula would be beneficial. Second, removal of the mask of denial and focus on institutional bias within states (Gerstenfeld 2013). This can happen by repealing policies that do not coincide with spirit of inclusion. Lastly, Gerstenfeld (2013) recommends focusing on reducing prejudice in society. Given our history, this is probably the most difficult. However, the use of the media and social networks for mass distributions of public service denouncements of hate and promotion of intergroup tolerance may begin to change the value system that rewards intolerance. With respect to law enforcement, recent scholarship has unveiled some ideas as to how to enforce and reduce hate crime offending at the community level. Frielich and Chermak (2013) suggest in pop guide no. 72 a series of general considerations and specific responses to reduce hate crimes. For instance, they recommend training police officers, responding to victim needs, increasing police presence, monitoring hate groups, and tracking incidents, reaching out to minority communities and engaging educational institutions and mass media. They also note that treating hate crimes as regular crimes has limited effectiveness. For offenders convicted of hate crimes, programs such as "Think Again" in the U.K. that focuses on cognitive transformation to reduce recidivism from preliminary findings appear promising as a rehabilitation alternative. Taken together, these recommendations may address the historical significance of hate crimes and the unintended consequences of contemporary hate crime statutes.

References

Freilich, J. D., & Chermak, S. M. (2013). *Hate crimes* (p. 72). Problem-oriented guides for police: Problem-Specific Guides Series.

Gerstenfeld, P. B. (2013). *Hate crimes: Causes, controls, and controversies*. Sage.

Grattet, R., & Jenness, V. (2001). The birth and maturation of hate crime policy in the United States. *American Behavioral Scientist, 45*, 668–696.

Mason, G. (2014). Legislating against hate. *The Routledge International Handbook on Hate Crime, 59.*

McDevitt, J., Levin, J., & Bennett, S. (2002). Hate crime offenders: An expanded typology. *Journal of Social Issues, 58*(2), 303–317.

Petrosino, C. (1999). Connecting the past to the future hate crime in America. *Journal of Contemporary Criminal Justice, 15*(1), 22–47.

Appendix

FBI Bias Indicators

Objective Evidence That the Crime was Motivated by Bias

An important distinction must be made when reporting a hate crime. The mere fact the offender is biased against the victim's actual or perceived race, religion, disability, sexual orientation, ethnicity, gender, and/or gender identity does not mean that a hate crime was involved. Rather, the offender's criminal act must have been motivated, in whole or in part, by his or her bias. Motivation is subjective, therefore, it is difficult to know with certainty whether a crime was the result of the offender's bias. For that reason, before an incident can be reported as a hate crime, sufficient objective facts must be present to lead a reasonable and prudent person to conclude that the offender's actions were motivated, in whole or in part, by bias. While no single fact may be conclusive, facts such as the following, particularly when combined, are supportive of a finding of bias:

1. The offender and the victim were of a different race, religion, disability, sexual orientation, ethnicity, gender, and/or gender identity. For example, the victim was African-American and the offender was White.
2. Bias-related oral comments, written statements, or gestures were made by the offender indicating his or her bias. For example, the offender shouted a racial epithet at the victim.
3. Bias-related drawings, markings, symbols, or graffiti were left at the crime scene. For example, a swastika was painted on the door of a synagogue, mosque, or LGBT center.
4. Certain objects, items, or things which indicate bias were used. For example, the offenders wore white sheets with hoods covering their faces or a burning cross was left in front of the victim's residence.

© The Author(s) 2017

F.S. Pezzella, *Hate Crime Statutes*, SpringerBriefs in Policing,
DOI 10.1007/978-3-319-40842-2

5. The victim is a member of a specific group that is overwhelmingly outnumbered by other residents in the neighborhood where the victim lives and the incident took place.
6. The victim was visiting a neighborhood where previous hate crimes had been committed because of race, religion, disability, sexual orientation, ethnicity, gender, or gender identity and where tensions remained high against the victim's group.
7. Several incidents occurred in the same locality, at or about the same time, and the victims were all of the same race, religion, disability, sexual orientation, ethnicity, gender, or gender identity.
8. A substantial portion of the community where the crime occurred perceived that the incident was motivated by bias. Version 2.0, 2/27/2015 7.
9. The victim was engaged in activities related to his or her race, religion, disability, sexual orientation, ethnicity, gender, or gender identity. For example, the victim was a member of the National Association for the Advancement of Colored People (NAACP) or participated in an LGBT pride celebration.
10. The incident coincided with a holiday or a date of significance relating to a particular race, religion, disability, sexual orientation, ethnicity, gender, or gender identity, e.g., Martin Luther King Day, Rosh Hashanah, or the Transgender Day of Remembrance.
11. The offender was previously involved in a similar hate crime or is a hate group member.
12. There were indications that a hate group was involved. For example, a hate group claimed responsibility for the crime or was active in the neighborhood.
13. A historically established animosity existed between the victim's and the offender's groups.
14. The victim, although not a member of the targeted racial, religious, disability, sexual orientation, ethnicity, gender, or gender identity group, was a member of an advocacy group supporting the victim group.

Index

© The Author(s) 2017
F.S. Pezzella, *Hate Crime Statutes*, SpringerBriefs in Policing,
DOI 10.1007/978-3-319-40842-2

CPSIA information can be obtained
at www.ICGtesting.com
Printed in the USA
BVOW07s0829050217
475328BV00006B/230/P